RELIGIOUS PARADIGMS IN THE NOVELS OF GRAHAM GREENE AND BRIAN MOORE

RELIGIOUS PARADIGMS IN THE NOVELS OF GRAHAM GREENE AND BRIAN MOORE

By

Dr. Samuel V.T.

DISCOVERY PUBLISHING HOUSE PVT. LTD.

NEW DELHI-110 002

Published by:

Tilak Wasan

DISCOVERY PUBLISHING HOUSE PVT. LTD.
4831/24, Ansari Road, Prahlad Street
Darya Ganj, New Delhi-110002 (India)
Phone: +91-11-23279245, 43764432
Fax: +91-11-23253475
E-mail: parul.wasan@gmail.com
discoverypublishinghouse@gmail.com
info@discoverypublishinggroup.com
web: www.discoverypublishinggroup.com

***First Edition:* 2011**
ISBN: 978-81-8356-730-5

Religious Paradigms in the Novels of Graham Greene and Brian Moore

Printed at:
Shree Balaji Art Press
Delhi

PREFACE

At the outset, it would be appropriate to trace the context in which I came in contact with the fictions of Graham Greene and Brian Moore. My life in the Order of the Imitation of Christ as a monk and a major Seminarian enabled me to get the grasp of the ritualistic life of the church and the theology that nourishes it. Then my experience as an expatriate teacher in Ethiopia at the time of Socialist revolution put me in direct contact with a Marxist government in an orthodox Christian country and its repercussions in the social, political and religious life of the people. The total revolutionary background and the insufficiency of life and the missionary endeavours of Catholics that are described in many of the novels of Graham Greene and Brian Moore could all be experienced in a turbulent East African nation in the violent period of their history. Thus it was that I decided to writ my doctoral thesis on Brian Moore who was ardently appreciated by Graham Greene as "my favourite living novelist", and Graham Greene who was looked upon by Brian Moore as his spiritual mentor.

Cardinal Newman in his The Idea of a University denies the possibility of a Catholic Literature. According to him if literature is to be made a study of human nature, we cannot have a Christian literature. It is a contradiction in terms of attempt a Sinless Literature of a Sinful man.

But Graham Greene and Brian Moore, by analyzing the secular foundations of Christian psyche point to the possibility of a Christian literature in the background of Catholic church.

Both of them detect the loss of religious sense and a proportionate loss of the dignity of human action. They point out the need of a cause, religious or political to go on. They concentrate on the failing men, for in failure man reveals himself as he is and is not taken up with contented complacency. Both writers cherish a spiritual sense of glory. Glory should not be sought in military grandeur or fame or ambition, but has to be realized privately as a discreet virtue, particularly, in solitariness, resulting in a transformation from rational to ethical and to an irrational action. To the contending factions of religion and politics, as well as to the process and formation of upright will and the redemption from bad faith in interpersonal relationship, the one and only panacea recommended by both of them is faith, a faith in action. Both the novelists in their common philosophy of life justify and substantiate the logic of a comparative study of modern protagonists portrayad in the real as well as fictional milieu of life.

In this study, the works of both the novelists, particularly the religious novels, are reduced to a single isomorphic unit of experience against the background of the Catholic Church which is counted as the towering and tantalizing monument wherein the protagonists either find solace or fumble. The analytic approach adopted here is based on the critical principles of the Readers Response theory.

This thesis is comprised of five chapters. Chapter 1 - Introduction provides the biographical backgrounds of both Graham Greene and Brian Moore, summarily explains their complementing nature, as well as the critical theories applied in the analysis that ensues. Chapter 2 - Suffering-the seed of paternity, elucidates the varying suffering protagonists in the initial phases of both the novelists and how they transform this suffering, later, for the noble cause of the soul. In Chapter 3 Art as Agape - what genuine Christian Self emptys and why many men of genius in Art, Science and Architecture end themselves in predation, are explicated.

In Chapter 4 - The Willing Spirit and the Weak Flesh-man's need for a redeeming grace in the context of rampant bad faith, even in the face of a miracle in modern life is brought out. In Chapter 5, Zest – the Flavour of Life-the muddled state of affairs of an industrialised urbanised society in its drab, routine life is depicted. Chapter 6- Conclusion-summarises the salient points from the theological reflections of great theologians elucidating the pattern and life discussed so far.

Dr. SAMUEL

ACKNOWLEDGEMENTS

I wish to take this opportunity to express my deep gratitude to all those who have served as the major and minor premises in the practical logic of the formation of this thesis.

The work is carried out under the guidance of Dr. Maya Dutt, Reader in the Institute of English, University of Kerala. In madame's highly integrated personality I found a real guide, friend, and philosopher. But for this sincere and serious person in her scholastic bent of mind and persuasive skills and tactful approach this thesis would have been an impossibility. I cannot but stand stupefied when I remember of her magnanimity and earnestness in bringing two critical texts from Canada while she was on an educational tour there. Her sincerity earnestness and dedication shown while going through each page of this thesis leave in my mind an unerasable mark of a real guide who will serve as a model to refer in my academic career.

Dr. Radha, the Professor and Head of the Institute of English, University of Kerala and Dr. Jameela Begum, the Director of the Canadian Study Centre, University of Kerala, who provided me with all the original and critical materials from the department and Dr. Jancy James, the director of Comparative Literature, Institute of English, University of Kerala, for providing me with the psychological insight in this comparative work are gratefully remembered. Without these galaxies of strong will and enlightened brains behind me, this thesis would have remained in the embryonic sack of desire covered in the casket of diffidence.

I express my profound gratitude to Bethany Ashram – Order of the Imitiation of Christ (the cradle of the reunion movement in India) in providing me with a theological as well as philosophical training.

I am thankful to all Librarians and Libraries for rendering me access to materials. I wish to thank, especially, St. John's College Library, Anchal, Mar Ivanios College Library, Mar Theophilus Training College Library, Kerala University Library, Institute of English Library, The British Council Library, Eloor Library, Library of Bethany Ashram, Trivandrum, The Canadian Centre Library at the Institute of English, Kerala University and CIEFL Library, Hyderabad. I am singularly grateful to the Shastri Indo-Canadian Institute, New Delhi for providing me with all the details of Brian Moore's works.

I should acknowledge my thankful indebtedness to Dr. George and Dr. Rani George of the Polymer Science Department of Cochin University for their valuable contribution by lending me the books with theological insights.

All my well-wishers and benefactors in the Department of English at Anchal St. John's College and Mar Ivanios College are remembered here in gratefulness and cherished memories.

The typists and printers of Computer Techniques, Kumarapuram and Jayamatha Technical Institute, Nalanchira are gratefully remembered, for I could bank on their diligence, promptness, energy, time and good will in the formation of this thesis.

Dr. SAMUEL

CONTENTS

1 INTRODUCTION

Religion and literature are inextricably linked. For religion links man to God and to other men. These metempirical and empirical dimensions of experience and interaction are to be expressed, for human unity, in language. The harmony that language sets is unique to man in the whole of creation. Self-awareness, reason and imagination have disrupted the harmony which characterizes animal existence. Reason, man's blessing, is also his curse. It forces him to cope ever-lastingly with the task of solving an insoluble dichotomy. Having lost paradise, and his unity with nature, he has become an eternal wanderer (Ulysses, Oedipus, Abraham, Faustus). He is impelled to go forward and with ever-lasting effort to make the unknown known. He is driven to overcome this inner split tormented by a craving for absoluteness. Thus, this dichotomy of man's existence generates needs which far transcend those of his animal origin. In this thirst for unity, in the first place, he tries to construct an all inclusive mental picture of the world which serves as a frame, a reference, from which he can derive an answer to the question of where he stands and what he ought to be. But such thought systems are not sufficient. If man were only a disembodied intellect, his aim could be achieved by a comprehensive thought system. Since he is an entity endowed with a body as well as a mind, he has to react to the dichotomy of his existence not only in thinking but also in the process of living, in his feelings and actions. He has to strive for a totality and perfection in all spheres of his being in order to find a new equilibrium. Devotion to an aim or an idea or a power, transcending man, such as God, is an expression of this need for completeness in the process of living. This experience, and search for the one is universal. That is why even those who have detested religion as the "metaphysics of the masses" have found meaning in religious allegories and myths. The expression of this internal unity in human inter-relatedness is essentially literature. The diversity and dichotomy of our existence is in search of a union, a form in language. That is why literature is named as "sacrament of encounter".

This search for a religious experience of the human predicament was much felt in the nineteenth and twentieth centuries. John Galsworthy, G.B. Shaw and H.G. Wells came out with stiff objections to traditional techniques and themes. The obsession of the themes of novels with a particular social milieu and the dramatic technique of narration so far followed with a setting and a denouement was denounced. Novelists discovered the importance of ideas. They decided to make the novel a powerful instrument of moral suggestions, the social indictor, the vehicle of understanding, the instrument of self-examination, the parable of morals, the criticism of laws, institutions social dogmas and ideas.

The Bloomsbury Group, headed by Virginia Woolf through stream of consciousness technique, led the novelists to an absorption in the mental processes. James Joyce introduced psychological elements very powerfully. Sigmund Freud and Carl Jung rationalised the subconscious and the unconscious. Jung went even to the extent of rationalizing the subconscious and unconscious instinctual drives. What was so far preserved as a sacred serenity wrapped up in superstition and myth, was demythologized and the mind became naked. In the outside world the warmongers of Europe barked at each other in their power-crazy madness. The world lost its balance, security and sleep. Materialism and uncertainty and lost self images were the facts to be grappled with by the writers.

When stream-of-consciousness limited the mental realm in the field of writing, the disrupted, distorted, disgusted ego of man that often longed for a death-in-life, turned to the anchorage of religion for a moment's silence and calm, for the sap of life and for a pellucid vision. The pioneer among these writers was Graham Greene, who has confessed that Brian Moore is his "favourite living novelist". Thus novelists, from the evocation of fragile, atavistic states of tendency to revert to the spirit, turned to judgements served on the spirit in its relation with the deity. In the nineties those who doted on the symbolic and the evanescent, turned eventually to Roman Catholicism. Graham Greene and Brian Moore complement each other as representing the outside and the inside view of the Catholic Christianity. Hence, the relevance of this comparative study.

Graham Greene testifies to the inherent relationship between his life and novels in the following words:

> If there are recurrent themes in my novels, it is perhaps only because there have been recurrent themes in my life. Failure seemed then to be one of them.[1]

This declaration by the author himself constitutes an invitation to examine and explore his life and living. Regarding his autobiography - *A Sort of Life* (ASL) - he writes: it is much the same motive that had made me a novelist, a desire to reduce the chaos of experience to some sort of order and a hungry curiosity (ASL 9).

All this order seeking chaos of experience has its basis in his childhood days. Graham Greene, the fourth of the six children of Charles Henry Greene, was born on 2nd October, 1904. His pre-school days had unpleasant experiences that found its loud thinking in his autobiography. Whether "it is the memory of sitting in a pram at the top of a hill with a dead dog lying at his feet" or "the man running furiously into a house to cut his throat, all cry for rescue like the survivor of a shipwreck" (ASL 13, 15).

His school was a place where "the misery of life started" (ASL 11). Berkhamstead School, where his father became headmaster, was "a savage country of strange customs and inexplicable cruelties" (ASL 54). The family moved to the school house, but Graham Greene was dispatched to St. John's, a boarding house. He writes "one was an inhabitant of both the countries, on Saturday and Sunday afternoons, of one side of the bai'ze door, the rest of the week, of the other. He asks: "How can life on a boarder be other than restless?" (ASL 13). He developed a sense of "Continuous grime" towards life.

The years of boredom in adolescence made him seek 'ways of escape'. He pondered over cutting his right leg or committing suicide. He writes: "Successful suicide is often only a cry for help which has not been heard in time." Though his cry was heard at the right time and he was saved from "the final act of rebellion" (ASL 62) he was convinced that "even drowning was preferable to the ignoble routine of school" (ASL 63). After resorting to several sorts of escapes like drinking a large quantity of hypo, draining a bottle of hay-fever drops, swallowing twenty aspirin before swimming, he went into hiding on the common. For this he was sent to Kenneth Richmond, a London-based psycho-analyst. And he writes, after a six-month stay with Richmond, "I had emerged from my psycho-analysis without any religious belief at all, certainly no belief in the Jesus of the School Chapel" (ASL 93). In the initial days of Oxford he was "a muddled adolescent who wanted to write but had not found his subject, who wanted to express his lust, but, was too scared to try, and who wanted to love but hadn't found a real object." (ASL 87-88)

These baffled desires ended in a desperate longing for his brothers' nurse and the waitress at St. George. After this "for years he could take no aesthetic interest in any visual thing . . . he was fixed like a negative in chemical bath." (ASL 93). The war against boredom turned him to experiment with a revolver. He thought to "enjoy again the visible world by risking its total loss" (ASL 94) and to play Russian roulette with the revolver. Then he got disgusted and turned to alcohol and one term of Oxford was spent in this drunken mood.

After his formal education he was plunged in indecision. He derides himself "I was hemmed in by a choice of jails in which to serve my life imprisonment" (ASL 106). Thus from the British-American Tobacco Company to The Times, it was a deliberate flight for survival. In the vehemence of tension and ennui he longed for a holiday and he did the absurd by allowing the dentist to pull out a perfectly good tooth for a whiff of ether. "A few minutes unconsciousness was like a holiday from the world. I had lost a tooth, but the boredom was for the time being dispersed." (ASL 113)

Greene did not remain on The Times for long. But he had already written his first novel when he was on the 'Nottingham Journal'. Greene was engaged to be married to Vivian, a Roman Catholic Girl. His primary difficulty at that time was "to believe in a God at all" (ASL 120). Greene was converted to Catholicism in February 1926. It was a turning point in his life.

The accounts of his life so far described reveal that Greene was constantly trying to escape. In his naughty absurd way he was trying to transcend the existential "encompassings" to reach a more harmonious, tenable world. Though he admits "a loss of memory" (ASL 120) regarding the arguments of His existence, he was in search of a God. As R.W.B Lewis observes: . . . the religion to which he was converted was deeply modified by the personal experiences that flanked the conversion direct and personal responses to deal with".[2]

Though the converted Catholic framework influenced him much in the christocentric and theocentric elements in his works, there were other goading factors in his literary career. From his fathers optimism rooted in Robert Browning, he took a different view. "Fathers enthusiasm for Robert Browning was the bacillus of a recurring fever, but it was not a belief in God that Browning confirmed" (ASL 84). Thus Greene was trying to condition himself from a new angle for his nourishment for life and literary career. The following lines from Browning's "Bishop Blougram's Apology" is the befitting epigraph for all his works:

> Our interest is on the dangerous edge of things
>
> The honest thief, the tender murderer
>
> The superstitious atheist, demi-rep
>
> That loves and saves her soul in new French books
>
> We watch while these in equilibrium keep
>
> The giddy line midway. (ASL 84)

This is a realm rooted in the raw life of men and not simply a blind ejaculation of "God is in his heavens and all is right with the world."[3]

Another major influence that shaped his mind was Marjorie Bowen's *The Viper of Milan*. He writes:

> "Anyway she had given me my pattern. Religion might later explain it to me in other terms, but the pattern was already there—perfect evil walking the world where perfect good can never walk again." (ASL 17).

This struggle of the ignorant armies of good and evil is dominant even in his last phase of writing and even religion ceases to be a sufficient "hint of an explanation". He writes: "with the approach of death, I care less and less about religious truth, one hasn't long to wait for revelation or darkness." (ASL 121). In response to Evelyn Waugh's taunting remark on his drift to faithlessness in 'A Burnt-out Case, Greene quoted Browning:

> All we have gained then by our unbelief
>
> In a life of doubt diversified by faith

For one of faith diversified by doubt

We call the chess board white-we call it black. (ASL 84)

But between the two extremes symbolised by the "white" and "black" squares of the chess board, Greene was searching for an explanation for our inescapable condition of the burden of suffering and the ambiguity of human act—"the dangerous edge." This uniform search, into the problems and solutions, reflects the depth and breadth of this thesis. The philosophical and theological reflections that run through the Greenland is systematized in this work under the title *Theological Gestalt*. On human suffering he writes:

> The sense of unhappiness is so much easier to convey than that of happiness. In misery we seem aware of our own existence, even though this may be in the form of monstrous egotism. This pain of mine is individual, this nerve that winces belongs to me and to no other. But happiness annihilates us. We lose our identity.[4]

In A Burnt-out Case he identifies himself with Christianity ". . . the search for suffering and the remembrance of suffering are the only means we have to put ourselves in touch with the whole human situation. With suffering we become part of Christian myth". (LR 85).

Much prior to this theological and religious identification there are evidences to show that he longed for a unity in faith. He writes "People must have something outside the narrow world to live for, whether it is the idea of the inevitable progress of the proletarian revolution or just that a black cat will bring them luck if it crosses their path" (LR 85).

From this transcendental tendency of mind he emerges into a broader view after his Mexican travel. He confesses:

> "The world is all of a piece, of course it is engaged everywhere in the subterranean struggle . . . between the two extremes of pain and – God knows the opposite of pain, not we" (LR 33).

In his travelogue he discloses that "Life was happier with the enormous supernatural promise than with the petty social fulfilment, the tiny pension and the machine made furniture" (LR 49). With yearning for a fulfilment he looked for "a nearer the beginning" in any revolution, whether in Africa or Liberia. Africa with its demonic dances and cruelties represented to Graham Greene "a strangeness, a wanting to know".[5] The naked horror and primitive savagery of Liberia were causing an emotional conversion on Greene. He writes: "It was like a conversion and I had never experienced a conversion before" (JM 213). His African journey and its document Journey Without Maps, reveal that he had been torn between the paradoxical horn of faith . . . and it resulted in a "distrust of any future, based on what we are" (JM 30). He was tossed between "the belief that life should be better than it is and the belief that when it appears better it is really worse" (JM 32). This duality of mind, its conversion and the possibility of its anchorage in belief make "Greeneland" a cross-cross of the overlapping boundaries dividing right and wrong, good and evil, heaven and hell, the sacred and the profane and make it difficult to catch Greene, the secret spy and the double agent, in Greeneland. It is the territory of the mind, that is disturbingly close to the real world, a battleground of conflicting loyalties and certainties and across this braise door, Greene in his pensive mood watches the clashes of the ignorant armies by night and tries to deduce the epistemological, ethical, moral and theological conclusions for us.

In the presentation of the humdrum reality, Greene is so elusive that Edward Sackville West calls Greene "The electric hare whom the grey hound critics are not meant to catch."[6]

What I am proposing to do in this work is to bring out the theological gestalts as configurative points in his novels, particularly in his later "religious novels". Man as a microcosm in a macrocosm as in a ceaseless longing for a cosmic humanity that can be the shock absorber of all those limitations that the soul desires to fly from. The part's urge for the whole in Greene's *The Heart of the Matter*, in *Brighton Rock, A Burnt-out Case*, in *The End of the Affair* and in *The Power and the Glory* is analytically sought after in-depth in juxtaposition with the earlier as well as the later novels of Brian Moore – *The Cold Heaven, Black Robe The Colour of Blood, The Lies of Silence, Catholics, The Great Victorian Collections, The Temptations of Eileen Hughes*. The earlier novels are indirectly referred to as the steeping stones of the authors, in their search for a transcendence.

In this search for a theological gestalt author has taken critical support from great critics like Harold C. Gardiner, A.J.M Smith, Robert A. Wichert, Caroline Gordon Evelyn Waugh, Charles J. Rao, John Atkins, David-Price Jones, W.J. Weatherly, and V. Ivaseva in Twentieth Century English Literature: a Soviet View, insofar as they help to discern the protagonist's search for a cosmic ego in their sociological interpretations of the novels of Graham Greene.

II

Though Brian Moore has not written an autobiography, his life, vision and literary enterprises are supplied by critics, and interviewers. From the codified data of his life and works, it can be easily realized that there are many elements that justify this comparison with Graham Greene. Graham Greene appreciated Brian Moore as "my favourite living novelist."[8] Brian Moore's bewailing of "a lack of listening to the voice of the call" (BR VI) in the perilous and barbarous life of the Hurons and Iroquois reminds us of Graham Greene's prophecy of a "nearer the beginning" in the African and Mexican turmoil. The Catholic superstructure from which they look upon life as well as their concentration on the "losers" of life and failure make them vehemently complementary in nature. As we have seen Graham Greene's opinion on "losers", Brian Moore too feels: "failure is a more interesting condition than success. Success changes people, it makes them something they were not and dehumanizes them in a way that leaves you with a more intense distillation of that self you are" (BMCS vii).

Like Graham Greene, Brian Moore too transcends from secular to religious faith in his writings. When Greene became the centre of a religious controversy he came with a confounding statement "Religion is important as atomic science is".[9] In other categorical statement he stated:

> People must have something outside the narrow world to life for whether it is the idea of the inevitable progress of the proletarian revolution or just that a black cat will bring them luck if it crosses their path (LR 55).

Brian Moore too states in his interview with Ray Comskey: "I have always been interested in the fact that people must believe in something, nuclear disarmament, love as a regenerative force, politics, anything" (BMCS XV). Later, he grows in his interpretation of belief; he says: "when I discuss belief, I discuss it as a question of what stops us from the 'accidie' of despair, of saying we are only here to produce our species" (BMCS XV).

Just as Graham Greene does in his religious novels, Brian Moore too views religious faith as a form of belief.

> I found, when I started to write, I became very interested in the question of faith . . . the virtue of having a belief in something, I began to see and to feel, as I do now, that the great lack of modern life is the lack of a belief in something greater than ourselves (BMCS XV).

Such similarity of conception and religion in both these authors compel us to scrutinize their biography too. The ensuing brief sketch of the life and career of Brian Moore will certainly enable us to get the coherence in juxtaposing them in a comparative study.

Brian Moore was born in Belfast, Northern Island, on August 1921. Like Greene, he too was the fourth child in a family of nine. His father, James Brian Moore FRCS, was a surgeon at the Mater Hospital in Belfast. His mother, Eileen McFadden, came from Donegal. His father had married when he was fifty and died when Moore was eighteen.

Moore's household atmosphere greatly prized academic success and it was also engulfed in the aftermath of depression. Owing to this, academic achievement was considered the safe route to a respectable career and prosperous standard of living. The ambition of his parents to see him get through at school was thwarted by his weakness at Mathematics and he left school to join the Air Raid Precaution Service (ARP) at the beginning of the Second World War. The Emperor of Ice-Cream, reflects the experience of adult world that he had confronted in the ARP.

Though he was a drop-out, the ethos of St. Malachy's Diocesan College and Ardath College was chewed in the Belfast novels, particularly in the *The Feast of Lupercal*, his second novel. In this "very harsh", clerical and old-fashioned scholastic atmosphere, he too might have been cowed to submission, not allowing him to get maturity like Devine Darmund.

While a teenager, in the 1930s Moore became mildly involved in the left-wing politics, sold Socialist Appeal on street corners and joined the Belfast Theater Guild. So by the time he wrote Revolution Scripts and presented 'The Catholics; as a dramatic success, Brian Moore manifested the grip of reality as well as the spirit of change and revolution.

His service as a civilian employee of the British Ministry of Transport, provided him with opportunity to be in Algiers, Naples and Marseilles in the crucial moments of war. At the end of the war, again he found a job in UNCRRA (The United Nations Commission for Resettlement of Refugees). Thus he travelled to Warsaw, then as a free-lance writer to Scandinavia and France. Just like Mexico and Africa inspired Greene to write. *The Power and the Glory* and his travelogues, Brian Moore, though in quite another manner was preparing for his novel *The Colour of Blood* from his travel to Warsaw, Scandinavia and France.

After a short respite in England, immediately after the World War, he left for Canada. His eleven years in Canada gave him time for serious fiction as well as for proof-reading and reporting. In order to write his first novel, *Judith Hearne*, he lived for several months in a log cabin in the Lawrentian Mountains. Though he is a Canadian citizen and has sometimes been identified as a Canadian novelist he has lived in the United States since 1959. He went to California to write the script for a film for Alfred Hitchcock, and later became an adjunct professor at UCLA, eventually settling in Los Angeles.

Though there is no autobiographical support for his visions and life experiences that contributed to the growth of his literary career, his Irish background and his constant reiteration of Belfast Catholic, intellectual, and social milieu from an outsiders point of view take us to an authorial omniscient view. He had been brought up under the stifling weight of the Catholic Clergy; had been in left-wing politics and world war and had the experiences of travelling through the length and breadth of European country. He lives in the New World and Canada. This universal phase of his living is demandingly asking for the past life, the men and women in clash and clamour for a living, for the blooming of their personality at least in a foreign soil, if not in their own society. The clash and din and loss of the protagonists against a right religious, social, intellectual climate are compared here with the losers of the protagonists of Graham Greene. But more than a negative approach, the work deliberately looks into the creative mode. The Belfast protagonists, like Judith Hearne, Darmund Devine, Ginger Coffey, Gavin Burke, Mangan, Dr. Maloney, Bernard Macauley, Sheila Redden as well as Joseph

Andrews, Raven, Pinkie and Conder of Greene's fictions are looked upon as tending to an insatiated cosmic fulfilment in "a great presence" and getting nauseated in the end. This the unfulfilled search for a transcendence in empirical and metempirical dimensions is brought out in both the novelists. In this search for a belief, for religious faith and for moral questions both the novelists take three stages: complete rejection of Catholicism in the early novels; an investigation of the values of personal secular belief in the middle period, with which beliefs, the author gradually becomes disillusioned, and finally a return to an open interest in Catholicism. The "isomorphic unit of experience" that Green and Moore dwell on derives its sap from catholic life and search for a cosmic humanity rooted in catholic faith as a criteria for perfection and personal fulfilment.

III

This introduction will be wanting, if the critical theories and tools used in my investigation are not presented.

Sigmund Freud's article on "Michael Angelo's Moses" in 1914 in the newspaper "Imago" was a clarion call for analytic study on artists after their works. But, later, Carl Gustav Jung argued against this practice and showed that art and literature are not simply a therapeutic outlet of literary men, instead they are the creative essence based on beauty, brought out realistically at the moment of adoration of beauty. Thus psychological criticism began to search for that process in which emotion and idea consummated in a new issue of beauty. Literary criticism thus emerges in offshoots like, existentialism, structuralism, phenomenalism and Gestaltism based on gestalt psychology.

In the present work I use Gestalt criticism to bring out the "patterns" of life that are elucidated in the novels of Graham Greene and Brian Moore. Scholars of psychology find patterns equal to a "gestalt" in English language. A picture that seems to be beautiful and appropriate to the mind, is a Gestalt. The forms, qualities and events of the world may produce life centred pictures in the mind. This is named as Gestalt. Man's mind is filled with such types, patterns or pictures. In this constant picture building process of the mind, some may elicit much emotion, some may lead to constant questioning. Some may be the beginning of something, some may be seen as an end. Some may be forms of revolution, some stand for change. The revolutions in Mexico and turmoils in Africa led Graham Greene to the pattern of a "nearer the beginning". Brian Moore in Huron land sought for the "unheard voice of conscience". These responses to life, form pictures that are varied. Thus Gestalts are divided into Open Gestalt, Closed Gestalt, Living Gestalt, Changing Gestalt, and Dead Gestalt.

What I am concerned with here is the models or forms of life in both the novelists' fictions. The similarity and difference of these forms draw our mind to a symmetry that contributes to its aesthetic aspect. Then the significance and the unity of these aesthetic forms of life is brought out in each chapter referring to the realistic and theological setting in which they are moulded. What is singularly noted while supplying gestalt critical principles in determining the various chapters of the book is the principle of co-relatedness and not mere co-existence: forms and their co-relatedness. Consider, for example, Gavin Burke's clash with the world:

> . . . shivering between the cold linen sheets of his bed, staring into the darkness, he felt the unseen room whirl, then grow still. His life since leaving school had been a see-saw. . . . In both worlds, lack of purpose, lack of faith, was the one deadly sin. In both worlds, the authorities, defecting that Sin, arranged one's punishment. All of Life's races are fixed and false you stand at the starting line, knowing you can run as well as others, but the authorities, those inimical and unknown arbiters, have decreed that you will not get

> off your mark. They know, those authorities, that your place is with the misfits that your future will be void.[10]

Raven's and Pinkie's world is with the misfits. Thus there is essential correlation, though all are creations of different authors.

By bringing forth the life projected by these forms and their co-relatedness through experience and emotion in a mystical act, our heart is getting identified with the form and transferred into the reflected form of the object. Thus the christfigures of the unknown whisky priest, the Abbot in *Catholics*, Cardinal Bem in *The Colour of Blood*, and Fr. Laforgue in *Black Robe* are identified, compared and evocatively discussed with the help of the Gestalt and Reception critical tools.

The life projected by these gestalts or forms and the acts and experiences of the senses and the circumstantial and culturally created acts in the creation of the protagonists mix us together to get the sights, beauty and knowledge and thus the mind gets transferred in the reflected form of the object. For example "the bad-faith", 'nausea" and "alienation" of modern men are pictured in the protagonists of Moore's Belfast novels as well as in Greene's *The Man Within*, *The Heart of the Matter*, *The End of the Affair*, and *A Burnt-Out Case*. The genius behind these phenomena, and the medium - the cultural and religious - and the meaningful dimension in which it is made effective in the peruser's mind, are differentiated and identified by the receptionist and gestalt criticism on a practical level by the use of the principle of "verisimilitude".

Graham Greene's portrayal of a real world as it is in the realistic realm of life creates a seedy, drab, fever-stricken world, where the individuals are not merely grouping in darkness, but searching for an oasis, either in a perfect humanity or through faith in God. He sketches out this search in such a way that we are warned of our identification, and mental norms, in our search for transcendence. The tension terrain of Brian Moore creates those protagonists who are constantly dismayed and annoyed by the questions "why am I here?" and "what am I here for?" Thus in experiential description of the world, both unite in the form of the world to convey that little patch of life - the nature grappled by this world is human nature - in its varieties, deprivation and differentiation from the original. The shape of this difference of life, and deformity of human nature is subjected to the emotional movement and intellectual creativity by both the novelists. It is brought out by probing into the "isomorphic unit of experience" from a catholic back ground in the fictions of Graham Greene and Brian Moore.

IV

The theological patterns or gestalts that we search for, are analysed by the critical tools of reception or reader response criticism. The division of the book into "Suffering-the Seed of Paternity," "Art As Agape", "Zest the Flavour of Life", "Willing Spirit and the Weak Flesh", is based on the forms and themes conveyed by the novels in a Catholic framework. But after categorising the religious novels of Graham Greene and the later novels of Brian Moore, the themes and their theological colour are brought out through the role of "the implied reader" and "the literary repertoire".[11] By "implied reader" the author means a standpoint which allows the real reader to assemble the meaning of the text. Thus the readings of *The Power and the Glory*, *Black Robe*, *Catholics* and *The Colour of Blood*, are viewed from the positive point of view of religious zest as "springing water of grace from inside" and also from an ascetic angle in the chapter "suffering" - where the protagonists are giving themselves up physically and mentally for a spiritual paternity. The elements of reality and the allusions to the world outside and the inside world of the protagonists are distinguished to bring out the social, historical and cultural norms to elicit reaction to the text on its way of making the "book a machine to think with" (CC 263). The lieutenant in *The Power and the Glory* and Daniel in *Black Robe* are contrasted with the unknown whisky priest and LaForgue to develop "discernment" and "sagacity" in the readers (CC 249). The Lieutenant's search for the priest and the invitation of a priest to get the confession of his prey, creates a transformation in the reader; so too Daniel's loud refusal of the European possession mania and his forsaking of the missionary priest in the adoration of a new culture challenges the reader to be sane in his own culture.

The social, historical and cultural norms and their differences are brought out in the staunch attitude of the Marxist lieutenant, the Algonkin-African belief, and the monastic dedication in *Catholics*.

In the chapter entitled "The Willing Spirit and the Weak Flesh" Greene's *The End of the Affair* and Moore's *Cold Heaven* are discussed with the help of the "defamiliarising technique" (CC 251) of Reader Response Criticism. Sarah and Marie Davenport are poles apart in their "Bad Faith". Sarah's conversion is a theological achievement whereas Marie Davenport's search for pleasure leaves us with the idea of an inextricable link between world and virtue in resolving conflicts and the purpose for which it should be resolved. In this *Catholic* and modern social reality the familiar background is produced, but parts are altered and the frame of reference is changed. Social and secular validity is negated in the theme of sainthood and miracle; and through these negations both the novelists lead us to a greater realization.

In "Creation as Agape" the ideal characters of the protagonists in *A Burnt-Out Case* and *The Great Victorian Collection* are juxtaposed as artists who have fallen upon the thorns of life and bleed. What challenges the reader is the dichotomy and paradox of the heroes. From the pull of the absurdity of life and delimiting factors, an analytical attempt in the meaningful dimensions of creativity is worked out.

dichotomy and paradox of the heroes. From the pull of the absurdity of life and delimiting factors, an analytical attempt in the meaningful dimensions of creativity is worked out.

Author agrees with Iser's consideration that "a book is a machine to think with" (CC, 263). "The principle of contrast or reverse" (CC, 266-67):

> That is, an idea, a norm, or an event can only take on its full shape within the reader if it is accompanied more or less simultaneously by the negative form as recommended by Iser for the easy comprehension of the book, is employed in all chapters (CC 255).

And the author has shown these negative forms in the levels of story, characters, plot and technique. The opposed poles of town and country, the inside and outside of Church life, the real conversion and the suspended belief, the absurdity and nothingness of life, sufferings of real paternity are brought out to show that these novelists are leading us to real "situational thinking" (CC 279).

REFERENCES

1. Graham Greene, *A Sort of Life* (Harmondsworth: Penguin, 1977) 454. Further references to this edition will be indicated in the text by the abbreviation ASL followed by page number.
2. R.W.B. Lewis, *The Picaresque Saint* (1956, London: Gollancz, 1969) 225.
3. Kenneth L. Knicker Bocker, *Selected Poetry of Robert Browning* (New York: The Modern Library, 1951) 3.
4. Graham Greene, *The Lawless Roads* (1939, Harmondsworth: Penguin, 1976) 85. Further references to this edition will be indicated in the text by the abbreviation LR followed by page number.
5. Graham Greene, *Journey Without Maps* (1936, Harmondsworth: Penguin, 1978) 37. Further references to this edition will be indicated in the text by the abbreviation JM followed by page number.
6. Philip Stratford, *The Portable Graham Greene* (1973;

Harmondsworth: Penguin, 1977) vii.

7. Brian Moore, *Black Robe* (London: Palladin, 1987) V. Further references to this edition will be indicated in the text by the abbreviation BR followed by page number.
8. Jo O'Donaghue, *Brian Moore: A Critical Study* (Montreal: McGill Queen's UP, 1991) 2. Further references to this edition will be indicated in the text by the abbreviation BMCS followed by page number.
9. Sameul Hynes, (ed.) *Graham Greene. A Collection of Critical Essays.* (New Jersey: Prentice-Hall, 1973) 173.
10. Brian Moore, *The Emperor of Ice-Cream*, (London: Andre Deutsch 1966) 192. Further references to this edition will be indicated in the text by the abbreviation EIC followed by page number.
11. Seturaman, V.S. (ed.) *Contemporary Criticism: An Anthology* (New Delhi: Macmillan, 1989) 252. Further references to this edition will be indicated in the text by the abbreviation CC followed by page number.

2 SUFFERING – THE SEED OF PATERNITY

Man as a being is a becoming to the exigencies of excellence imbued in his soul. But a search for the modes of self-realisation or self-actualization corresponding to the "entelechy" or form of each ones' being generates creative and constructive geniuses. This tension of self-realisation can be marred by existential tensions generated by the positive or negative values in interaction. Thus, vaulting ambition, or indifference or passivity perpetuated by an indifferent society, insufficient father figures, the absence of positive strokes, a highly puritanic society that merely perpetuates parochialism, masochism or patriarchal or matriarchal dominance, may distort the ego of both the vision of the form and the means to follow it. Schopenhauer remarks:

> In every individual the measure of the pain essential to him was determined once for all by his nature, a measure which could neither remain empty, nor be more than filled . . . if a great and pressing care is lifted from our breast . . . another immediately replaces it, the whole material of which was already there before, but could not come into consciousness as care, because there was no capacity left for it. . . . But now that there is room for this it comes forward and occupies the throne. Each individual bears within himself a disruptive contradiction; the realized desire develops a new desire and so on endlessly.[1]

He adds:

> From where did Dante take the materials of his hell but from our actual world? And yet he made a very proper hell out of it. But, when on the other hand he came to ascribe heaven and its delights, he had an insurmountable difficulty before him, for our world affords no materials at all for this. . . . Every epic and dramatic poem can only represent a struggle, an effort, a fight for happiness, never the enduring and complete happiness itself.[2]

All systems and all religions try to soothe man in this tragic plight by advocating many ways of escape. Samuel Hitchman, the founder of Homoeopathy says that there is a radical itching in man, may be from the time of disobedience in the garden of Eden; and this inadequacy postulated as "psora, psyphilis and psychosis," has its telling in the physical malady of men! For Wordsworth we are here "trailing clouds of glory" and "the child is the father of man." Pascal found man as a "thinking reed" and William Blake concludes that "innocence is lost in experience." Self-awareness and "*Nishkama Karma*" are propounded by *Gita* to master the suffering existence of man. Sri Buddha concluded that "desire is the root of all *dukkha*" and after a prolonged study on "*Prathithya Samudpada*"—the inherent ingredients of our present suffering—affliction is found to be a fact and to wipe it out, *Moksha* in *Kaivalya* is suggested. Christianity counts on it as a fact and Jesus says realistically, "if any one would come after me let him deny himself and take up his cross and follow me."[3]

Novelists like Graham Greene and Brian Moore in their earlier as well as later fictions have explored the causes of this existential problem and point to the possible points of sublimation in the daily routine of life.

The description of the tragic sufferings and afflictions of man take different colours in the fictions of Graham Greene.

Whereas Brian Moore portrays the preterition and perversion of individuals through institutions—particularly Catholic ones, Graham Greene substantiates the dictum of William Blake that "innocence is lost in experience". Innocence sitting alone invites suffering. This sinless suffering of the innocent, here and now, has dominated the early novels of Graham Greene. In Brian Moore these protagonists are not "determined" characters, but free to act, however in their lack of a person or a cosmic image to guide them, their freedom ends in "free-doom".

In *The Man Within* and *A Gun for Sale*, the horror of domination changes the innocent protagonists to anguish-ridden characters. Dixon comments:

> "What elicits human horror and indignation is not so much the suffering that the strong may with courage endure, as the suffering at random inflicted upon the weak and innocent and defenceless."[4]

Alfred Adler the Viennese psychiatrist, while propounding the "purposive point of view" in his Individual Psychology states that "an individual is more influenced by his expectation of what will happen to him in future than what has happened in past."[5] Together with this "fictional finalism"[6], the individual has to cope with "superiority strivings", "inferiority feelings", compensation of social interest, life style and "creative self". All these are the warring elements in the minds of the protagonists of both the novelists.

The protagonists of the earlier novels of Graham Greene and Brian Moore clearly lack the primary support in their purposeful image-making, the insecurities within the family and inappropriate father figures as well as a society that do not extol their life style or creative self, stand in the way of their growth. Religion, which should be a social outlet for the inadequate ego, aggravates the malignant growth of their self. The Catholic Church in which the protagonists are reared is frustrating either in the form of their desire to become priest as in case of Pinkie, or in providing rigid social and ethical life and leave the individual to mere devotionalism that does not touch their ego, as in the case of Judith, or by stunting their intellectual growth through the excessive demand of a system as in the case of Brend Tierny.

Once this felicity for merging with a cosmic ego that can very well anchor the ego in a rational and in an equilibrium of emotional life, is lost, the earthly father figures and society become simply mere puny figures to support the growth of an integrated personality. In Pinkie, Raven, Joseph Andrews and a host of others in Greene's novels, this is what occurs and Brian Moore is only adding to this fact in the protagonists of the Belfast novels.

The sheer materialism and the ennui of a mechanical society breed artificial social interactions that lead the individual in the terrain of struggle and suffering. *England Made Me*, *Brighton Rock*, *The Heart of the Matter*, *A Burnt Out-Case*, *The End of the Affair*, *It's a Battle Field*, *The Man Within*, *The Honorary Consul*, *Our Man in Havana* and *The Bomb Party* are case studies in point. *Beatrice in Our Man In Havana* remarks: "I don' care a damn about men who are loyal to the people who pay them, to organisation . . . I don't think even my country means all that much . . . would the world be in the mess, it is if we were to love and not to countries."[7]

In the epigraph to *The Honorary Consul* taken from Thomas Hardy, Greene says: "Things merge into one another – good into evil generosity into justice, religion into politics. Even religion is an attraction to the forbidden fruit."[8] Fowler in *The Quiet American* remarks:

> We make a cage for air with holes, I thought, and man makes a cage for his religion in much the same way – with doubt left open to the weather and creeds opening on innumerable interpretations. My wife had found her cage with holes and sometimes I envied her.[9]

In the same tenor Bernard McAuley admonishes Eileen in *The Temptation of Eileen Hughes*: "Gods are like the Sun. you can't get too close. They'll burn you. God's don't like you to get cheeky . . . you may not be wanted. You may not be goodenough.[10]

Thus, finding that suffering is an indispensable part of life, from "the dangerous edges" of life both the novelists transform suffering for a noble cause in realizing spiritual paternity. Greene's *The Power and the Glory*; *Monsignor Quixote* and *The End of the Affair*—where a sinner is brought to sainthood through a converted life—and Moore's *The Catholics, Black Robe*, *The Colour of Blood* explicate this truth. Life is a terrain of terror for Greene and the dark force of suffering escapes his grasp; but all the same it is a great grim force. In Brighton Rock, when the little waitress Ross tells Pinkie, "Life's not so bad," Pinkie turns to her vehemently, "I will tell you what life is. It is jail. It's not knowing where to get some money. Worms and cataract, cancer, you hear' emshrieking from the upper window-children being born. It's dying slowly."[11]

But suffering differs as individuals and experiences differ. *In The Man Within* – the very first novel, the dichotomy of the within and without cramps Andrews down to a nothingness. His panicky stride, uttering "dangerous", "dangerous" and his taking shelter in Elizabeth's cottage seem to have been done in "a wave of self-pity passed across his mind and he saw himself friendless and alone, chased by harsh enemies through an uninterested world."[12] His betrayal of Carlyon terminates the last link of friendship and the excruciating dichotomy haunts him.

> He was, he knew made up of two persons, the sentimental, bullying, desiring child, and another more stern critic. . . . Always while one part of him spoke, another part stood on one side and wondered. 'Is this I who am speaking? (MW 24).

> There was nothing in him, but sentiment, fear and cowardice, nothing in him but negatives. How could any one believe in, if he did not even exist? (MW 25)

After the betrayal to the authorities a gang of smugglers, previously led by his father: "a sense of overwhelming desolation passed over him; a wonder whether he would ever know peace from pursuit, and he gave an unconscious whimper like a rabbit snares" (MW 27). "Loneliness and fear were like the emptiness of hunger to his belly" (MW 40). As he tells Elizabeth "It is as though there are about six different people inside me. They all urge different things. I don't know which is myself" (MW 188).

He blames his father for his cowardice and irresolution. "My father and mother made me. I didn't make myself" (MW 52). In answer to Elizabeth's question as to why he came to a smuggler's life he retorts: "My father did it before me" (MW 57). Thus Andrews is unconsciously avenging himself on his father but he always discovers wanting: "And all the time I was at sea, I could see how they wondered that such a mountain could bring forth such a mouse (MW 71). He felt "a sort of Judas". Later in his alienation he sleeps with Lucy and takes the responsibility of Elizabeth's suicide, to identify himself with the man within. On an errand of supreme importance", he hacks himself to death.

An inadequate father figure and a lost childhood leave Andrews with another man within him, that is angry with him. This is the agony of the first hero of Graham Greene, who is an epitome of a split personality.

Andrews is simply the beginning of an array of characters who are eaten up by existential anguish. Pinkie of Brighton Rock is another boy who is activated by an inadequate childhood. After Kiate's death he inherits the leadership of a gang of racecourse hoodlums. Fred Hale, who had been given away to a rival gang was distributing the Kolly Kibber cards. When he had been spotted by the boy, he took refuge in the company of Ida Arnold. But Hale is missing in the gap of a wash. Fred is killed when Spicer places the card in snow's restaurant. The boy goes for it. When he is caught by Rose, he marries Rose and murders Spicer while Ida's net closes on him, he enters into a fake suicide pact with Rose, but blinded by his own vitriol, he dashes over a cliff and is "whipped away into zero-nothing" (BR 243).

We remember Pinkie: ". . . his gray eyes had an effect of heartlessness . . ." (BR 8). "The word murder conveyed no more to him than the word "box 'collar', giraffe" (BR 45). "There was poison in his veins" (BR 68). ". . . the horror of the world lay like infection in his throat" (BR 205).

Raven in *A Gun for Sale* is betrayed by Anne in whom he puts all his trust and he gets confirmed in his belief that "there was no one outside your own brain whom you could trust: not a doctor, not a priest, now a woman.[13] In his nightmare of evil he concludes, "This is not a world I'd bring children into" (GS 121). In his harelipped condition, there has always been war for him.

The melancholic world which he has had to bear with is revealed when he murders Cholmondley:

> Raven shot him with despair and deliberation, he shot his last chance of escape, plugged two bullets in where one would do, as if he were shooting the whole world in the person off stout moaning bleeding Mr. Davis . . . there was no other way; he had tried the way of confession and it had failed him for the usual reason. There was no one outside your own brain you could trust: not a doctor, not a priest, not a woman (GS 168).

Arthur Rowe, the protagonist of *The Ministry of Fear*, lives in haunting fear. In a dream he talks to his dead mother "people want to kill me because I know too much."[14] In the *The Third Man Harry Lime*, the shadowy racketeer, betrays his distorted humanism "In these days old man, nobody thinks in terms of human beings, Governments don't. So why should we?"[15]

To Dr. Hasselbacher we are alienated ones, for he says: "You should dream more, Mr. Wormold. Reality in our century is not something to be faced" (QA 10). Fowler in *The Quiet American* is not at all grateful when Pyle saves his life in the Viet-Minh ambush" "I hadn't asked to be saved, or to have death so painfully postponed." (QA 110). This is the fundamental state of mind of Greenes heroes—all in the grip of existential nausea, anxiety, uncertainty and absurdity.

In *It's a Battlefield*, the battlefield becomes the central metaphor of the novel. In this world of commerce, the heart is tossed between loyalty and betrayal, love and lust. Jim Drover is petitioned. But the prolongation of Jim's release causes disturbance and Conrad sleeps with Milly, love degenerates to lust and shameful remorse. Then betrayal gives place to the murder instinct. In the ensuing chase for the Police Commissioner Conrad is knocked down by a car. Milly is left to the absurdity of life when her husband comes out of prison. The mechanical London life is represented in Kay Rimmer's match-box factory which is: "A hand to the left, and hand to the right, the pressure of a foot."[16]

In *The Heart of the Matter*, Scobie's human ego, that is wrapped up in pity and sentiments, is in obvious conflict with an indoctrinated sacramental ego. "Pity in the lack of an ascetic morality leads him to self-destruction, emotional imbalance and spiritual degradation."[17] The great mental tension that Scobie feels when he finds it difficult to keep Louise happy – the "awful" vow that he had made at Ealing's marriage is shattered after fourteen years of married life. A divided ego, an unfulfilled vow and a changed feeling, shadow his ego. His absence at the death-bed of his daughter, Catherine, gradually fills him with remorse and guilt which can only be atoned by his deliberate presence at the death of the child in Pende. He feels one never really missed a thing. "To be a human being one had to drink the cup" (HM 118).

Scobie's overriding sentiment also vitiates his moral and family life. Greene shows this scathing power of sentiments when he writes: "A man open to bribes was to be relied upon below a certain figure, but sentiment might recoil in the heart at a name, a photograph, even a smell remembered" (HM 53-54).

He yields to the sentimental demands of his wife to be away. It is not a matured decision; neither the purpose of sending her away, nor the means he adopts to bear the expense and his subsequent involvement in diamond smuggling and his relation with the Jew Yusef makes Scobie aware of his moral degradation. Then, even the "Our Father who art in Heaven" becomes a mere matter of routine and the absolution of the confession box – "They were a formula the Latin words hustled together – a hocus pocus" (HM 154).

The split personality and the divided ego are what we see in his affair with Helen. He knows that the affair is sinful, but he cannot end it. In this connection it is appropriate to recall what St. Paul says: I cannot do the good which I think to be good, instead I do the evil, which I prefer not. Scobie falls in desperation; even a confession box doesn't give him any consolation:

> When he came out of the box, it seemed to Scobie that for the first time his footsteps had taken him out of sight of hope. . . . It seemed to him that he had left for his exploration the territory of despair (HM 213-214).

His personality crumbles with the "slow disintegration of lies", which he uttered to his wife and in the inexorable pain of a spiritual loss he feels as if "he had exiled himself so deeply in the desert that his skin had taken on the colour of the sand" (HM 226). The fact is that the internal ego is fully conscious of the sentimental weakness. "Do I, in my hearts of hearts, love either of them, or is it only that this automatic terrible pity goes out to any human need and makes it worse?" he wonders. (HM 198) He is lost between his love for Helen and his pity for Louise. He turns to prayer, but it lies "as dead on his tongue as a legal document" (HM 181). He prefers death to the unhappiness of his two ladies.

His sacramental theological self pained him at the communion and he pretended a pain in his chest. But when Fr. Rank comes down from the altar bearing God in his hand he prays "Oh God, I offer up my damnation to you; take it. Use it for them, and he believes now that his soul is damned for ever" (HM 217). The sacrilegious communion leads him to unimaginable mental agony. He pictures God appearing to him with "a bleeding face, of eyes closed by the continuous shower of blows: the punch-drunk head of God reeling sideways" (HM 228).

The murder of Ali by Yusef augments his feeling that he is a catalyst of evil and he takes recourse to the step of suicide. But then the Catholic consciousness counts it as "Unforgivable Sin'. An earlier attempt at Bamba ended in malaria and a nightmarish vision of a departure. "Suicide was for ever out of his power—he couldn't condemn himself for eternity—no cause was important enough (HM 89).

But in his mental balance suicide is regarded as much better than continuing in sacrilegious acts. He counts it as "a continuous shower of blows" rained on the bruised face of Christ. Intense is the moment, the emotion, the act. He studies the symptoms of angina pectoris so that his death may appear natural and kills himself with an overdose of the Evipan tablets prescribed by doctor for an unknown symptom. He plans and conceals it perfectly in his last act of pity—destroying some of the entries made in his diary.

And what a choking and revealing experience he has when God's voice tries to restrain him:

> Can't you trust me as you would trust a faithful dog? I have been faithful to you for two thousand years. All you have to do now is ring a bell, go into a box, confess. . . . If you live, you will come back to me sooner or later. One of them will suffer, but can't you trust me to see that the suffering isn't too great (HM 250).

Scobie's suffering, thus is the conflict of his ego and the indoctrinised-ideal ego.

It is a moment in which existence precedes over essence. Though essence, in the form of divinity and sacramental sense, comes forward to for prominence, the overriding influence of existential anguish and the sense of bedimmed personal glory give place to self-assertion, in taking all the responsibility on oneself.

This negative "fictional finalism" motivates an individual who is bound to any system in life. The positive thrust that a society must confer on an individual is lacking in the first novels of Graham Greene and that is the cause of the internal angst and conflict of the protagonists of the first novels of Brain Moore too.

Judith Hearne is a bleak and powerful depiction of a lonely middle-class catholic. Everywhere in this powerful book there is loneliness and despair. The excessively detailed descriptions of Judith's room is the filtering of her gloomy consciousness:

> A chair, broad-beamed, straight backed, sat in the alcove by the bay window an old pensioner staring out at the street. . . . Across the worn carpet was a wardrobe of brown varnished wood with a long panel mirror set in its door . . . while beside the gas fire a sagging, green-covered armchair waited its human burden. The carpet below the mantel piece was worn to brown fibre threads. She hurried on, passing over

> the small wash basin, the bed-table with its green lamp, to reach the reassurance of her two big trunks black topped, transbound, ready to travel.[18] (JH, 19).

For her the Catholic community of which she is a part is merely an organized religion. In the church affairs she follows the dictums of her Aunt rather than her conscience:

> No she had followed her aunt's lead in that. Church Affairs, her aunt once said, tend to put one in contact with all sorts of people whom one would prefer not to know socially. Prayer and a rigorous attention to one's religious duties will contribute far more towards one's personal salvation than the bickering that goes on about church bazaars. (JH 58-59)

When this advice serves its negative impact on her she finds the lack of a social outlet, in a Church, where community, charity and sharing are vehemently stressed. And she distances herself from the Catholic laymen, though their role is greatly stressed by the Vatican Council. Aunt d'Arcy's friends the professional elite simply elicit an illusory feelings of superiority in her.

In the emphasis of communal prayer at the expense of personal prayer the Catholic clergy fosters docility and devotionalism to a particular saint and it becomes the whole religion for Judith. Thus Judith's oleograph of the sacred heart is a talisman that goes everywhere with her; and her needs are projected on it. The sacred heart becomes a combination of best friend, councillor and "terrible judge". But as the novel progresses Judith falls victim to drunkenness and the triumvirate role of the sacred heart crumbles and she falls into unbelief. She demands a sign and is not successful.

After her rejection by James Madden, no consolation is left and religion becomes an observance. Just like in Scobie, "The Our Fathers and 'Hail Marys' stumbled through her mind, repeating themselves until they were meaningless, as hurried and without devotion as the mumbled response of the altar boys" (JH 139).

The confessional box does not show any sympathy and repeats the traditional advice of priest:

> Now, you listen to me, go home and sober up and examine your conscience while you are at it. You should be grateful that God hasn't punished you worse mortal sin on your soul and you not in a fit condition to receive absolution (JH 206, 207)

The Tabernacle, too fails. She is left with a mental picture and as Jenny Floods comments, she feels "the lack of a great presence". Lenehan and Miss Friel at the breakfast table and the priest Father Quigley represent "a compassionless society and compassionless Church." It is in grappling with this society and in interrelating with these arid men and women both in her intimate and social life that she loses her identity. A friendless alcoholic, Hearne at last ends in a breakdown only to be taken to the mental asylum.

The same type of social milieu is represented in *The Feast of Lupercal*. The clergy dominated system of education stunts the growth of personality. It imposes and perpetuates a sort of "religious apartheid". The violence in the class rooms which makes the pupils hate the masters and fight back by any devious means in their power; the inevitability of the masters becoming bullies, since only violence guarantees respect; the filth and squalor, depersonises him.

> He was a tall man, yet did not seem so: not youthful, yet somehow young; a man whose appearance suggested some painful uncertainty. He wore the jacket and waist coat of a business suit, but his trousers were sagkneed flannels. His black brogues classified with loud Argyle socks . . . . Similarly his hair, worn long and untidy behind the ears thinning to a sandy should on his freckled brow, offset the Victorian respectability of waist coat, gold watch-chain and signet ring.[19]

This description of Dev by Connolly is the gist of the angst ridden personality of Devine. The system does not allow him to reach emotional maturity. Devine relies on half truths, rationalization and self-justification.

> As for girls, well, he had never been a ladies man . . . It was the education in Ireland, damn it. He had been a boarder at this very same school, shut off from girls until he was almost a grown man. . . . (FL 5).

Devine had never really behaved an adult and this immaturity prevailed outside the campus of the school. When it comes to the point of going to sleep with Una, he is "sick as a boy who had not prepared: the role had been reversed, he was victim, he would be punished for his failure (148). He too turns to the moment of defiance where he asserts loudly "I am a grown man. I will not be treated like a school boy" (FL 228) and "I have been treated like school boy. A school boy" (FL 231).

This timid man offers Una as a sacrifice to his terror of scandal and the power of Catholic establishment in his life. The internal instability and timidity are adequately sketched out: "But I am liar, Mr. Devine remembered guiltily. No, not a liar I'm just trying to claim him down No sense upsetting him, is there? A little white lie never hurt anyone. "But what could I do? I didn't know what story to tell him. I had to say something (FL 157-158).

This timid, foolish and emanciated Devine is the product of a stifling imposition of a system. His "internal perceptual field" is rigid, narrow and stereotype dithering his personal growth, thwarting individuality. Devine Darmund, like Judith, suffers from an imposing society and their suffering in angst equates only in the protagonists of Graham Greene. In the terminology of Kurts Lewis, Devine undergoes an "approach-avoidance conflict" in his relationship with Una-She is both attractive and threatening. He becomes to maturity and personal decision in his selection of her but at the same time he is threatened of his social rooting in his catholic society. This is the cross on which he lies.

In *The Emperor of Ice-Cream* and in *The Lies of Silence* the personal angst that gnaws the moral and personal fibre of the protagonists is taking a social phase, in the protagonist's clamour for a purpose of life, for equality and justice in the world. The strong personal frustration is felt by Gavin Burke in *The Emperor of Ice-Cream*. "The whole bloody world was being blown up. But sally Shannon couldn't kiss him in front of a doctor" (EIC 135).

But he is not lost in this desperate internal perceptual field as in the case of Judith and Devine. Gavin Burke ventilates his feeling to the external world of war and reflects . . . His life, since leaving school, had been a see-saw, chapel, confessional and class room the catechism rooms. In both worlds lack of purpose, lack of faith, was the only deadly sin. (EIC 250). His father says "Oh Gavin". I have been a fool. Such a fool (EIC 260-61).

The same purposeless world is angered upon by Dillon in *The Lies of Silence*, on the morning of the second day, when he is forced to drive his bomb laden care to the hotel. Dillon thunders out:

> And now . . . Dillon felt anger rise within him anger at lies told over the years to poor protestant working people about the Catholics, lies told to poor Catholic working people about the Protestants, lies at rallies and funeral orations, and above all, the lies of silence from those in Westminster who did not want to face the injustice of Ulster's *status quo*. Angry, he stared across the room at the most dangerous victims of these lies, his youthful, ignorant, murderous captors.[20]

The whole of the Belfast furnished Dillon with a bruised state of mind on the first evening:

> He turned up towards Mill-Field, driving through those parts of Belfast which had become the image of the city to the outside world: graffiti-fouled barricaded slums where the city's protestant and catholic poor confronted each other, year in and year out in a stasis of hatred, fear and mistrust (LS 10-11).

The anger that Dillon feels on the morning when he drives through Belfast with a bomb in his car is due to the suffering perpetuated by a system. This is the loud clamour of a soul that is bruised by a tight social system and is butchered by the consequences of the same system. When he lacks the internal courage to face the reality, he wishes that he could supply that heroism:

> He had, instead, been put to the test by accident, a test he had every right to refuse . . . the moment he told them he was afraid, he would lose forever something precious, something he had always taken for granted, some secret sense of his own worth (LS 192-93).

This is the great suffering to which the IRA has led Dillon. Dillon is asked to take the bomb; any defiance means losing his wife. He becomes neurotic and the whole system bewails through him for liberation. Thus the past and the present stifle his artistic pursuit of poetry.

James Mangan's quest for glory in the poetic legacy of his alleged ancestor, James Clarence Mangan is born out of anguish as well as from an enthusiasm born of despair. The lost self-identity, the loss of his self-image and self-importance stem from his marriage to the film-star Beatrice Abbot. His lapse into an impecunious writer and her thriving to a promising artist leave him with a sense that he is nothing more than her husband' and the doorman's call "Mr. Abbot" brings the fact to our mind. Beatrice's departure compels him to latch on to the daguerreotype of his alleges ancestor, James Clarence Mangan for his identity. This failed writer and failed husband in his thirty-sixth year is in the firm grip of anguish and sense of alienation and search for control in the treasure of a past glory. But in the end he is deeply deceived in the poetic heritage and delves in to the past and tries to evade his own self; for the past exposes the qualities of his nature that he would not have preferred to know about.

Dr. Anthony Maloney in *The Great Victorian Collection* is in the cauldron of "approach avoidance conflict". The collection that he created out of his dream theaters his profession, aggravates the already disrupted family life, tossing even his mother to the side of suspects by calling him and his invention a "fake". In the agony to protect the articles of his dream and in his realization of his incapacity to dream another one of the same type that he created, he is gripped in despair. He falls in love with his secretary, Mary Ann, and indulges in sex and drink and relies on pills for sleep. Anthony Maloney represents "the rootless, alienated, essentially unloved" modern man. "The overdose, barbiturates combined with alcohol,[21] is a potent symbol of modern man's angst and the spiritual vacuum in which he lives.

If Anthony Maloney is eaten up by the anguish of an artist, Mary Dunne is caught up in a deep sense of guilt accruing from a false moral choice and its consequences. She is a "split personality" enmeshed in guilt resulting from her attempt to establish for herself "a rationally based humanistic form of secular happiness". The search for identity thus, is her cause of agony. In a natural way Mary Dunne talks to herself and explains to herself to forestall panic:

> But even as I raged against Ella Mae, I knew it had nothing to do with her, it was my hateful premenstrual tension that put in a lunatic anger against her, that started the trembling, that becomes a shaking, independent of me, as though my heart is an engine which suddenly comes loose inside me and will shake my whole body to pieces.[22]

Mary Dunne lacks control and she recognizes the neurotic side of her personality when she tells: "See, said my 'Mad Twin' he is avoiding you, he's not going to answer to you: Mow, stop that, warned sensible self" (MD 28-29).

She is guilty by association with her father. This guilt increases in her relationship with Jimmy, Mavkie, Hat Janice Solan and Ernie. In her admission of a father whose death haunted her adolescence, she confesses the depravity and sexual guilt. Her agony for an identity of personality at last finds an oasis in her dead father." May be I am not promiscuous, but I have been married three times and I am only thirty-two. May be without my knowing, I am old Dan Dunne's daughter after all" (MD 78).

Internal tension leads her to insanity and how terrible is her irrationality when she says:

> I looked at him (Terence) when he said that. Did he know? He Sat facing me, smiling, sympathetic, sipping at his coffee Did he know the Juarez dooms were on me . . . . I do not know what it is . . . I know only that I have done wrong, that I am being punished, that I will never be happy again (MD 248).

Her duality is dissolved in irrationality and isolation. And not an inch of her personality is spared from guilt.

The agony that Brendan Tierney faces in *An Answer from Limbo* is procured by his ambition. In other novels the main characters suffer alienation from society, family and religion and the intellectual milieu of the time. But here the predominance of ambition flinches him in Sin of omission and he deprives him of his wife and daughter. That ambition which operates as his motivation limits his "internal perceptual field' to a narrow rationalistic outlook and an indifference to the rest of reality. One of the early paragraphs exposes Brendam Tierney:

> For I have not become great. I who boasted that I would never settle for the ordinary evocations have settled instead for – What? . . . Yet the novel with which I hope to fulfil my prophesy lies in a drawer in my office, a loved but ailing child, its life engendered by my fitful labours . . . yet with no possible alternative routing, my course was set towards a destiny. I have not yet accomplished. In that dream I weep.[23]

Brendam, creating his life in the past and planning it future appears as an image of omnipotent. But this god fails in grappling the circumstances that confront him later: Thus frustration, alienation and desolation creeps in his life.

> When I leave my work room I enter in to a State of waiting. At home, I walk from room to room I pick up books but do not read them, I sit in a chair and stare . . . The apartment is blessedly peaceful; no rows, no children, no television. (AL, 224)

This intensity of dedication bears the mark of negligence and causes the victimization of Mrs. Tierney. Her narrow and parochial values nurtured in the traditional catholic piety and guilt are being questioned and prepare her for estrangement. She reflects:

> They were well named, she decided. The darlings. That was her private name for them, what with their darling this and darling that. Look at those back rests, would you. Brendan not thirty and her even younger. Back rests, as if they had one foot in the gravel. Bohemians, my eye. . . . On Monday I'll have the looking after of them. Then they'll see who's boss (AL 70)

The sense of powerlessness, despite her motherliness and nursing competence, is very strong. In a futile attempt to reach the telephone she dies of a paralytic stroke.

Mrs. Tierney's death and funeral set her apart from Brendan and betrays the moral vacuum exists in her. Thus disharmony caused by Mr. Brendan eats into the narrow of their family life and Brendan is an indifferent person causing agony to him and to all those who associate with him. It is ambition that destroys the domestic as well as the social life of Brendan Tierney.

Bernard McAuley's obsession with a "substitute gratification" to fulfil his physically impotent personality and to fill vacuum in the ex-seminarian's psyche are the central theme of *The Temptation of Eileen Hughes*. From Eileen's humble house in Church Street to a mansion in County Louth and the invitation of her mother Agnes are not works of charity but actions of a monomaniac. This cult of materialism and money as a means of pleasure lead to the obliteration of conscience and forgetfulness of self. For Mona takes refuge in sexual encounters with strangers. Bernard himself loses his faith. When he loses his vocation to be a religious man he loses his faith too. When he thinks he is going to die from an overdose of drugs, he betrays his life's despair. "Its all over between me and God. I offered myself to God once. I wasn't wanted" (TEH 158). Thus in the undeveloped spiritual life of Bernard McAuley, all characters loose their integrity and the right type of life. Obsession with a deprived virility deprives Bernard of the contact with the divine culminating in the slavery of fleeting realities of life and terminating in suicide.

After this glimpse into the causes of suffering in individuals, in the later phases of Brian Moore's novel, suffering, both physical and spiritual becomes an indispensable ingredient for spiritual maturity. Suffering as the seed and indispensable water of martyrdom makes its appearance in the latest phase of Brian Moore's fictions, too.

Catholics, *Black Robe* and *The Colour of Blood* bring forth the tension and suffering that is demanded from the divines in their ecclesiastical life fulfilment. Here Brian Moore is on a par with Graham Greene in theme and character, as well as in the theological dimensions of the society they are dealing with.

Black Robe is a fable for our world, insistently contemporary in its exploration of the conflict between religious faiths, or rival sorceries, as they must always seem to each other. In this novel Father Laforgue's suffering is both mental and physical and it reaches a macabre level causing horror and panic. But the journey is purely for a soul.

> It is travel of the most difficult sort the superior had warned him. Yet it is the most advantageous way in which to make the journey. For if you travel with a hunting party of men, women and children, there is always the change that, if a child or an adult falls ill enroute, a soul can be gained for God by a deathbed baptism. Father Brabant and others have written in The Relations that each time they journeyed to the Huron lands they had the great privilege of saving at least one soul in this manner. Remember such a blessing will more than justify all the perils and discomforts you may suffer. (BR 30)

Thus Fr. Laforgue's suffering is for a spiritual paternity of a race. He suffers the hostile world, hostile religion and severity of quarrels of the Iroquois:

It is a different set of people. The Unruly, unrestrained children, who even try to fondle his genitals and are not controlled and the fetid smell of savages lay like a cloud in the confined space and gradually he became aware of giggles as young girls and boys crawled about in search of each other. (BR 41)

Then Fr. Laforgue falls prey to the bigotry of Mestigot. The hunchback Mestigot considers him an agent of the devil demon and exercises his sorcery over Laforgue who evades him saying "I am not a demon."

In the Iroquois camp, Fr. Laforgue stripped of his clothes he is spat on his face and is made to dance. When he comes to the mission:

> I baptize you, in the name of the Father and of the Son, and of the Holy Spirit . . . He moved in, saying over and over the words to make them Christians and forgive their sins. Was this the will of God? Was this true baptism or mockery? Would these children of darkness ever enter heaven? (BR 223)

The already bruised psyche of Laforgue is shaken by a crisis in faith. His co-priest's martyrdom begets horror in his mind, still he answers 'yes' to the question of love. "he poured water on a sick brow, saying again the words of salvation. And a prayer came to him, a true prayer at last. Spare them. Spare them, O Lord . . . . Do you love us? . . . Yes" (BR 224).

The entire arduous journey and the agony of the within and without is for love. Cardinal Bem in The Colour of Blood suffers excruciating pain both from within and without. He confronts a three dimensional conflict. The primary source of his suffering is personal. He is a good man, modest and holy but above all moderate. The spiritual passage that he was perusing just before the first attempt on his life reveals that he longs for a contemplative life—a communion with pure reason.

> Do you think that a man born with reason yet not living according to his reason is, in a certain way, no better than the beast themselves? For the beast who doesn't rule himself by reason has an excuse, since this gift is denied him by time. But man has no excuse.[24]

In this extolling of the ideal of reason shown by St. Bernard of Clairvaux, Bem too longs to escape from the unreason of the world. In the next sentence we read: "Sometimes, reading St. Bernard, he could abandon the world of his duties and withdraw into that silence where God weighted and judged" (CB 2).

This meditation is juxtaposed with violence, where his driver dies and he escapes miraculously. From there he is caught in house arrest and then the long perilous journey always fearing the pursuers, and finally an attempt to inoculate him to death just before the martyr's day Mass are all for the final cause. Though he is successful in preventing the incinerating speech that will ignite rebellion and atrocities, he is shot by the girl who comes to take her communion.

His internal agony is intense, for he has to fight not against any enemy, but one of the factions of his own Bishops who has committed by religious dedication to obey him. When Bishop Krasnoy remarks:

> The nation in this critical time is like a great forest at the end of a summer of dreadful drought, a spiritual and moral drought. On the floor of this forest are millions of pine needles It takes only a spark to set them ablaze. (CB 164)

But the Cardinal is very sane in his thinking:

> I think our people are using religion now as a sort of politics. To remind ourselves that we are a Catholic nation while our enemies are not, to remind us that we always continued to be a nation even when the name of our country was taken off the map. It is all part of our collective memory and we cherish it. But what has it got to do with our love of God? (CB 166)

This statement evinces Catholicism as a badge of identity and also betrays political opposition. Such a wisdom is thrown into the abyss of guilt when he has to fight against the insurgent bishops. After the meeting he prays:

> I am your servant, created by you. All that I have I have through you and from you. Nothing is my own. I must

> do everything for you and only for you. Tonight at the meeting I was obsessed by politics. I thought of the danger of our nation. I did not think of the sufferings we cause you by our actions. My fault, my own grievous fault. (CB 18)

Thus the Cardinal is contrasted with three factors: the politics that he tries to lead in a conciliatory tone, the warring factions of his own clergymen, and the internal ego that is surging for a contemplative life. When such a wisdom and virtue is shot down we are not only "filling the gap" (as is demanded by the receptionist critics) between incidents, but filling a vacuum that exists among the ecclesiastical dignitaries. From the first shot in the initial pages of *The Colour of Blood* to the last shot when the cardinal spills his blood, while administering the Holy Eucharist, we are led to the question- what is the meaning of all this? What is depicted is the effect of the predominance of divine will over human will, just as in the case of the whisky-priest in The Power and the Glory. The price that the divines pay is for a spiritual progeny that must inherit the sanity, sanctity and sagacity of life.

This same conflict of the will is intensely elucidated in *Catholics*. Here Brian Moore brings out the theological net by sketching the life in the most primary unit of religious life.

The two novels that directly complement each other are Greene's *The Power and the Glory* and Moore's *Catholics*. In *The Power and the Glory*, the priest fails but not the priesthood. Despite his degenerate life, the priest is rooted in the missionary conviction. A secular priest is pitted against the Marxist Lieutenant whereas in Brian Moore's *Catholics*, the internal primary cells of the Church - the monastery and their renovation in the precepts and practices of faith are elucidated. If the former is a terrain of terror the latter is a terrain of tension. In *Catholics* the surrender of a will to a higher power is demanded - irrespective of age and experience of the Monk, but in the former, even life is lost and suffering for faith reaches the phase of martyrdom.

To look at the background, in the biographical note to *The Power and the Glory* the publishers write, "After journeys to Liberia and Mexico he wrote his two travel books *Journey Without Maps* (1936) and *The Lawless Roads* (1939) and also *The Power and the Glory* (1940)".[25] Thus Journey without Maps and The Lawless Roads unravel the tone of his mind and serve as a befitting study prior to the probing of The Power and the Glory.

The underlying tenet of *Journey Without Maps* is as follows:

> Today our world seems peculiarly susceptible to brutality. There is a touch of nostalgia in the pleasure we take in gangster novels, in characters who have so agreeably simplified their emotions that they have begun living again at a level below the cerebral . . . it is not, of course, that one wishes to stay for ever at that level, but when one sees to what unhappiness, to what peril of extinction centuries of cerebration have brought us, one sometimes has a curiosity to discover, if one can from what we have come, to recall at what points we went astray (PG 4).

Though from his infancy he has known the Catholic priests, the man and the office,

> Now, many years later as Catholic in Mexico, I read and listened to the stories of corruption which were said to have justified the persecution of the Church under Calles and Cardenas, but I had also observed how courage and sense of responsibility had revived with persecution – I had seen the devotion of peasants praying in the priestless Churches and I had attended Masses in upper rooms where the Sanctus bell could not sound for fear of the police. I had not found the integrity of the lieutenant among the police and

> pistoleros I had encountered – I had to invent him as a counter to the failed priest; the idealistic police officer who stifled life from the best possible motives: the drunken priest who continued to pass life on. (PG, 17).

The central debate is the antithesis poses in *The Lawless Roads* between religion and materialism in Mexico. The two views are embodied by the priest and the Lieutenant whose names are not given, so that the novel takes on the air of a parable as soon as the two protagonists are introduced and matched. Though the technique of a thriller, Greene gives his story a suspense. The action is one prolonged chase, strung round three meetings symmetrically arranged between the two men. Once even a casual survey on the background of *The Power and the Glory* reveals that Greene's concerns have taken a great stride of transformation from *The Man Within*, to *The Power and the Glory*. In the earlier novels he had been grappling with the sinful fallen man who has lost his anchorage in a society that is represented in It's a *Battlefield* and *England Made Me*. But by the time he comes to write *The Power and the Glory*, in his Catholic zeal, he is impelled towards a universal liberation, a thirst for salvation from the muddled uncerebral affairs of life. This paternal universal feeling is what we have seen in the former lines quoted from *The Lawless Roads* and *A Journey Without Map* which enshrine experiences of Greene prior to *The Power and the Glory*.

Similar are the formative influences on Brian Moore. In his fictional career, he is even indebted to Greene in his growth to protgononsts who stand for a spiritual paternity. In Black Robe he confesses that the writings of Greene on the Jesiut missionaries in Africa has been the inspiration for his Black Robe. Just like Greene in the earlier works, Brian Moore too in the initial works like the *The Lonely Passion of Judith Hearne, An Answer from Limbo, The Emperor of Ice-cream, The Last Temptation of Eileen Hughes, The Luck of Ginger Coffey, The Mangan Inheritance*, deals with the stifling sensation of the protagonists in a rigid Christian society and the tragic flow of mind and will that these protagonists bank upon and then pay with interest in loss of self and self-image. What is considered as a glimpse into the fact of faith in *Cold Heaven* and *The Great Victorian Collection*, seems to be taking on a definite shape of salvific spiritual paternity in *Catholics*, *Black Robe* and *The Colour of Blood*.

Greene has taken his hero through different scenes of fear and sacerdotal dynamism to intensify the theme of betrayal. The village where the priest has sought refuge and celebrated mass a second time, the prison, where the priest is charged with drunkenness, and finally through the arrest leading to his execution, Greene achieves the realistic growth of his hero. For the priest is tracked by a half-caste who forces him to return to a dying gangster - a catholic who might be saved by confessing. But the police have used him as an involuntary decoy in their ambush. The process of amelioration of earth is endurance, suffering, and the emptiness of giving, and it begins in the novel, here.

In his commentary, Steward Geen talks about the theme of *The Power and The Glory*:

> Greene selects his plot and characters to escape from whatever happens to be most boring in our day-to-day existence. It may be, however that the reader is less eager to escape from something. . . . From chaos to order, from a jumble of unpredictable and often incomprehensible sensations and experiences to a world wherein every part is clearly related to every other part, and the whole possesses reassuring coherence and unity. (PG 220)

In *The Lawless Road* Greene writes, Nobody can endure existence without a philosophy. This philosophy should be thoroughly satisfying, probably ought to recognize every human passion, to be intellectually defensible, and should appeal to what we consider our better nature. Graham

Greene's philosophy is Christianity as expounded by the Roman Catholic Church.

To differentiate the priest in his office and in his humanity, to place him in an environment of universal evil and to project him as a man of the flesh sharing the moral and human fallibility, though he is the divine of an "infallible church", the author has to take deliberate steps (1) to defamiliarise the priest, either from the shot ones or those who have betrayed priesthood (2) the poignancy of the tribulatory situations and the personal agony of the intimate personal relations have to be narrated and depicted sentimentally and rationally, and (3) at the same time the ameliorative function of the priest—the process of sowing the seeds of heaven—had to be continued. Thus a will, transforming and tantalizingly evading, at least spiritually, all human weakness in its mystical experience of a divine mission, and surrendering itself at the demand of life's termination, has to be kept. (4) Then again to save the protagonist from self-imposed asceticism—self-assertion, self-importance, self-search and confidence in ones activities become the root—must give place to self-acceptance of suffering when it is presented by life (5) Then too the secular kingdom that counts the search for a "celestical city", as merely a superstructure imposed on humanity as a threat and how that detrimental proposition - dialectical materialism - converts itself to annihilate the spiritual kingdom - has to be described. These are the functions which Graham Greene tries to bring home to the reader through this parable and its meaning. To elicit the reader's response he must keep the superiority of the reader in a Catholic verbal repertoire in the context of a Mexico, in a Marxist-Catholic confrontation. All this Graham Greene fulfils perfectly. In *The Power and the Glory* as in *Bread and Wine* the plot is episodic and consists of a succession of encounters "between the harried protagonist and a number of unrelated persons – while within that succession, we observe a pattern of three dominant and crucially meaningful encounters" (PC 223-34).

We first see the priest, when in disguise, sipping brandy in the office of Mr. Tench, the morose expatriate dentist. We follow him, episode by episode, as he is hidden and given food by Coral, the precocious daughter of an agent for a banana company, Captain Fellowes, and his miserable death-haunted wife; as he arrives in the village which is the home of the woman, Maria, by whom he has the child Brigitta; as he travels onward in the company of a mestizo, the yellow-toothed ignoble Judas who will betray him to the police; as he is arrested and released and fights his way over the mountains to freedom in a neighbouring state and the comfortable home of Mr. Lehr and his sister, German-American from Pittsburg, in charge of a mining operation; as he is enticed back across the border of Tabasco to attend the death of James Claver, an American murderer who has been fatally wounded by the police, is arrested again by the police lieutenant, taken back to the capital city and executed. Tench, Coral, Maria, the Lehrs, Calver—they are all strangers to each other. The episode with each of these thicken and expand the novelistic design (Coral, for instance, is the priest's good spiritual daughter, while Brigitta is his evil actual daughter).

The design is created by the three encounters. The first time, the lieutenant – whose whole energy and authority are directed exclusively to capture this last remaining agent of the Church – sees the priest and interrogates him; but he neither recognizes nor arrests him. The second time, the priest is arrested, but he is not recognized: the charge is carrying liquor. The third time, recognition is complete and the arrest is final. On separate, successive views of these incidents, paradoxical resemblances are registered about the two men. The priest disappears wearily into the interior, giving up a chance to escape in order to minister to a sick peasant woman, on the next page, the lieutenant marches by with a ragged squad of policemen, looking as though "he might have been chained to them unwillingly." Later on, he walks home alone, dreaming of a new world of justice, and well-being for the children of Tabasco there was something of a priest in his intent observant walk – "a theologian going back over the errors of the past of destroy them again" (PG 24). On the morning of his execution: "He felt only an immense disappointment because he had to go to God empty-handed, with nothing done at all (PG 210). "A few communions, a few confessions and an endless bad example' (PG 208). This wavering, undignified loyalty to his vocation makes him a genuine martyr.

Spirituality is positive. It is creativity. Creativity demands a departure from self-hood to an immaterial realm where all externality is fumed and fused into the alchemy of creation. Here the priest endowed with a divine mission of giving life, is tossed in the damned, satanic waves of revolution and is eaten up by suffering in the process of ameliorating human nature or incarnating God. A nameless priest amidst the unspeakable heat and the detonating beetles of Tabasco, sweating his way toward a sort of befuddled glory is of course the representative of the people and the lieutenant's proper adversary. But this journey is not for any mundane glory. The ruling that runs through the end of a War, and that essay on 'Vauven' is the search for glory.

> Glory is now a discredited word, and it will be difficult to re-establish it. It has been spoilt by a too close association with military grandeur, it has been confused with fame and ambition. But true glory is a private and discreet virtue and only fully realised in solitariness. Greene concludes: At certain moments the individual is carried beyond his rational self, on to another ethical plane, impulse which moves him to irrational action I have called the sense of glory.[26]

If he had abandoned priesthood like padre Jose he could live gloriously. If he had joined his daughter, he could save his daughter form a moral loss. Now he is a priest who has no possibility of a glorious and redeeming word on his character due to his worldly life. Why with all this he doesn't turn, from the trap of death? Why he doesn't stop the pistol from roaring? An unconscious suicidal tendency? No, absolutely No. That mystical surge of his soul which is saturated in the life of Christ and the life that is daily taking shape in his hand in Bread and the great conviction that the only solution to the universal evil is nothing but an incarnated God, and opening an avenue to incarnating God, daily; that is the intuition that impels him to the peak when he utters Hail Christ the King and falls prey to a bullet. Without loss of innocence one can be guilty. Society is a muddle. And the barbed wires of society cannot contain the radiation of the spirit. As the angel asked at the tomb of Jesus we too can ask after the death of the priest was it not right that he suffer all these and enter the glory. This identification of the spirit with the suffering and glorified Lord is the point of glory of the whisky priest.

Surprisingly enough the priest is a supreme paragon of modern invention of psycho-therapy. Hans Hofman, of the Havard Divinity School, for instance writes, in his *Religion and Mental Health*.

> It was only natural that Sigmund Freud should at the beginning of his career have thought of the irrational aspects of the human personality as chaotic and potentially dangerous powers . . . it did not occur to him that chaos itself may represent a very positive and fertile current of life. For the people of *Old Testament* especially in the creation story, the question was not: "Why is there chaos?" but rather "Why is there order?" For them, order was the outgrowth of daily living . . . The unique function of man, in their view, is to live in close, creative touch with chaos and thereby experience the birth of order.[27]

The chaotic subconscious of the priest and the society gets a fixed and ordered centre in the last cry of the priest

"Hail Christ the King". In a single individual, materialism is defeated, over-powered, sublimated, ameliorated and glorified through the adherence to Jesus the "élan vital" of the missionary zeal of the priest which is nothing but a universal search of all human being, at least at the pristine moment where spontaneity and impulsive behaviour gives place to cerebration. The anonymous priest is the supreme cerebration, which is the answer to this chaotic, evil and satanic might of the secular order and universal evil which is parallel to Brian Moore's lament over the African situation: "from the 17th century a voice is speaking, but not heard." The "negative capability" of Greene to amalgamate the darkness and the light, the evil and goodness and at the same time crown the individual with divine glory so as to repeat the biblical doctrine that "God had relegated man a little to angels" and created him as paragon of creation is dexterously achieved. Again, the dissatisfaction and discontent toward the vehement disproportionate, fanatic zest of a political hegemony to thrust its power over the primitive people is foiled. For at the sight of the priest the populace clamour for sacraments. Thus the corruption that the priest bears and the mission that he achieves escape dichotomy. Here is a people who had been in the dark and have now seen a light.' Jesus suffered and gloried but the church's mission continues. When the next priest knocks at the boys door, after the whisky priest's death the same mission goes on. The religious psyche, even in the political turmoil is a fact. It "broods over the chaos" as in Genesis and it gets its liberation in the priests – in the one who dies, and the one who comes.

To elicit the reader's response, Graham Greene, is a master-craftsman in adeptly and adroitly applying the dexterity to cajole and extol the factual existence by making him looking at the spontaneous impulsive behaviour, just to lead the reader to a cultured life of cerebration, which was the most cherished aim that he had manifested in Journey Without Maps. First he must retreat himself from the setting, by taking the rearguard of it and must get the direct co-operation from the person who is to perceive the innovation of the novelist. *The Power and the Glory* is a subjective objective innovation, for he writes in *Ways of Escape*:

> I had not found the idealism and integrity of the Lieutenant of *The Power and the Glory*, among the police and pistoleros I had actually encountered – I had to invent him as a counter to the failed priest: the idealistic police officer who stifled life from the best possible motives: the drunken priest who continued to pass life on. (PG 56)

As Wolfgang Iser says:

> Only when the innovations get against a familiar background that we get some idea of their novelty. Once the new is distinguished from the old, there arises a certain tension, because we have lost the security of the familiar. Thus without preconceptions and old assumptions the reader can approach the new and to get his mind transformed into the image created by the author.[28]

The corruption of the priest is a familiarising technique to emphasize on the operation of grace. Graham Greene follows this defamiliarising technique when the aura - the atmosphere, the circumstances, of his discovery is sketched out as a spot of universal evil, not only by the impulsive nature of the fragile human beings there, but in a coercive tension between the secular hegemony and the ecclesiastical superstructure. "Belief", "half belief", "non-belief" and the inordinate life of a priest are to be despised; so too the cruelties of the indoctrinated mad moderns of a philosophical doctrine are to be detested. Thus in the primitive, underdeveloped situation an unknown guardian angel of the soul is symbolically presented with a dentist (Mr. Tench) who is struggling with decaying tooth to replace them with new ones. His domestic superiority too is in jeopardy like that of the whisky priest for he is trying to flee away from wife and children. In the very first line the novelist is introducing us the tropicality of the situation and nature's callous indifference to the efforts of men.

> Mr. Tench went out to look for his ether cylinder, into the blazing Mexican sun and the bleaching dust. A few vultures looked down from the roof with shabby indifference, he was not carrion yet . . . It would not find anything there; the sharks looked after the carrion that side. Mr. Tench went on across the plaza. (PG 10)

Against this background of a moving dentist in a disorganized and dehumanised atmosphere; a priest too is introduced as a wanderer bearing the miracle of life in head, heart and hand. The author's work in mind was "the drunken priest who continued to pass life on. To present this "hound of heaven" he introduces the priest as a wanderer, who forgets I even his prayer book and scheduled voyage, on hearing the urgent need of his presence to dispense viaticum to the dying. When the priest is on the mule our mind is transformed from a man whose "dark suit and sloping shoulders reminded him (Mr. Tench) uncomfortably of a coffin, and death was in his carrion mouth already" (PG 12).

The stranger who sat with Mr. Tench "Sat there like a blank question mark ready to go, ready to stay, poised on his chair. He looked disreputable in his grey three-days' beard and weak: Somebody you could command to do anything" (PG 12).

Then suddenly, almost immediately we are transferred from the man to the priest – who is on the mule and our mind follows him. Through out the novel this transformation, this transcending travels occur. When he meets his own daughter who is on the brink of a loss, he is guilty that he fathered to a prodigal daughter, but then too he nurses to give eternal life to the harassed people a panicky slice of life.

The lieutenant too takes this strides of progress, in his fervent feverish fang of hunting, though often he too says "farewell to arms". Thus when he calls Padre Jose, the one who gave up priesthood, to hear the confession of the whisky priest, he too assumes a transcending figure in our imagination; a transformation from pistols to principles and then of course to the one in the halo of faith. Was it not a discovery by the champion of dialectical materialism that his system in its metaphysical jump of what philosophers acclaim from "is", to "ought" – what "is and ought to be". He is a priest and he ought to die as a priest. Is it not a moment when the Lieutenant is converted from a constructive genius - so far, he was that since he was sifting the last vestige of priests in the hideouts - to a creative genius, where the mind accepts superiority of faith and the last act in the struggle where the lieutenant is transformed into a distributor of sacrament, or at least a helper in the life giving process or a Simon to assist this Jesus - in the mission of distributing holy bread – to the Golgotha of life. We are changed and if we are not caught in the net of salvation "dull is our soul" as Wordsworth said in his sonnet years back, and we too may be sharing a pantheism not only with Wordsworth but even with the impulse induced by Iroquis of the Black Robe of Brian Moore. Our God may not be "The Manitou" - but other items of the fleeting nature. In this moment if *Trinity* is not revealed and if we are not baptized in the river of faith, we are caught up in the tragic lullaby of ignorance which claims God as *'Neti Neti'* For at the phase of incarnation of God in the iron heart of Lieutenant, all war-mongers hearts are ripped open to be filled in by the birth of satan as W.B. Yeats dreamt in a "The Second Coming". "The participation of the reader could not be stimulated if everything were laid out in front of him." (CCA 249) By an appeal to the "Sagacity" of the reader, a sense of discernment should be aroused. By this discernment, process of learning is stimulated in the course of which one's own sense of judgement may come under scrutiny. Thus attitude and reflection on attitude will follow. Then again participation, in the sensical, sentimental, aesthetic, noetic and moral realm should take place.

For the right response Iser proposes: The stratagems that should be followed, must be "negation", and keeping the superiority of the reader by creating "vacant pages" and through inviting the mind to fill the gap that exist in an occasion (CCA 255-58). From the outer appearance, and finally get the crux of the "within" getting aside the outward ones, by making the characters while adapting to new circumstances, unmasking their wordily corruption. When the lieutenant forgets the corruption of the priest and helps the priest to have a holy death we too forget the corruption and enter the extra-mundane dimension of existence.

To keep superiority, the author takes care to supply the reader with knowledge that is unavailable to the character and gives him a grandstand view of all proceedings and thereby makes the novel a medium to think with. There is an ongoing communication between the character and the reader in which the reader is asked to supply knowledge that is unavailable to character. In this processes the poignancy of the suffering of the divine is masterly sketched out. In the second chapter the reader is placed between the Lieutenant and the defeated priest; looking at the photograph the lieutenant said "He looks like all the rest". It was obscure but you could read into the smudgy photograph a well-powdered jaw much too developed for his age. The good things of life had come to him too early, the respect of his contemporaries, a safe, livelihood. The trite religious word upon the tongue, the joke to ease the way, the ready acceptance of other people's homage . . . a happy man. "A natural hatred as between dog and dog stirred in the lieutenant's bowels. "We have shot him half a dozen times" he said (PG 199).

When the moments of decision to search the priest approached, Greene writes:

> It infuriated him to think that there were still people in the state who believed in a loving and merciful God. They are mystics who have experienced God directly. He was a mystic too and what he had experienced was vacancy – a complete certainty in the existence of a dying, cooling, world, of human beings who had evolved from animals for no purpose at all. (PG 24-25)

Thus the reader is brought to the utter disbelief of the champion of the ruling segment and the iron will with which he is going to mete out the situation. The reader brings to the mind, utter dismay, uncertainty and the reader prepares himself for a catastrophe. But gap filling is not smoothly followed. For the reader is also placed against a priest who has lost his priesthood under the pressure of the rulers. The husband and wife talk of a poor woman who took to him her son to be baptized. She wants him called Pedro— but he is so drunk that he took no notice at all and baptised the boy Brigitta. Thus the author in contrasting Padre Jose with the whisky priest who still goes on in his way of life imparting and in this discovery the reader feels a superiority in the fulfilment of his emotive, cognitive search. Padre Joses' guilt and agony is again brought out in Bystanders. In the Lopez Tomb, Padre Jose was asked to pray before the coffin.

> They all watched him hungrily. "Padre Jose", the old man repeated. "A Prayer? It's impossible" he said. The Old man said, "You can trust us. It is just the case of a short prayer. I am her grand father . . . you can trust us" . . . Padre Jose said at last, "Leave me alone" . . . (PG 49)

Thus the reader who is left with a priest who has lost his self-image and plunged in the abyss of irremediable Judas' malady is called to discern a priest of the same cadre, of the same Church moving ahead, in staggering steps but with a steadied mind.

Our senses get stupefied when the whisky priest is tossed between amateurs and professionals searching for asylums at the door of Padre Jose gets the reply "go away go away".

> In the lamplight Padre Joses' face were an expression, of hatred. He said: "Why come to me? What should you think . . .? I'll call police if you don't go. You know what sort of a man I am". "Go", Jose screeched at him 'go'. I don't want martyrs here. I don't belong any more. Leave me alone. I'm all right as I am. (PG 112-13)

The grim pathos and agony scorches us when the priest quarrels with a bitch for a bone. "The priest had won: he had his bone. The bitch no longer tried to growl" (PG 140). This is another intense moment, when Greene invites to an orgy of imagination where primary imagination gives place to the secondary imagination just to give birth to an over mind or "over soul" which peeps into the agony that the "life givers" confront in this world.

Our imagination and intellect get it's meaning and image; it is no more "a dim analogue of creation". Here imagination becomes the medium of knowledge and art at the one and the same time. Here secondary imagination rooted in volition "dissolves, diffuses and dissipates" in order to recreate the lost and last image of Christ in the midst of parching humanity.

To reinforce the theological gestalt of missionary suffering the author brings heterogeneous ideas into fusion. He is a failed whisky priest who has, apparently no organisation in the moral side. For he fathers an illegitimate child and as a father, he is a failed one projecting out his physical failure Greene writes:

> The child stood there, watching him with acuteness and contempt. They had put no love in her conception, just fear and despair and half a bottle of brandy and the sense of loneliness had driven him to an act which horrified him and this scared shame-faced overpowering love was the result. (PG 142)

Man's goodness is not, the guarantee of God's presence. Though belief ends in good moral life, in the failure of man, in the corruption of man since he is a corporal being, who can utilize him but God? Trust in Him, and He knows how to make the stones utter Hossanna to him. Faith is a gratuitous gift, it is a leap into light since God is light. This illumination, enlightenment is the result of the suffering of the whisky priest as was the case of Job.

In *The Power and the Glory* the priest's suffering is salvific, escatholical and theological because his suffering is an act of love.

> The nobleness of Christ's passion is that it was not a work of asceticism, a sought after mortification, but merely the faithfulness of love. To accept and to offer inevitable sufferings in love is God's will. To impose on ourselves voluntary sufferings is to do our will and be reassured at small cost. Your crosses must come from your apostolic commitments and not from your personal fabrication.[29]

Our priest is the supreme paragon of this theological suffering, for several times he tries to avoid the catch by embracing different shelters and hide outs, but finally he had to succumb to what was thrusted on him. Thus, our mental gestalt is supplied to organise our mind, "a willing suspension of disbelief" has set in to pray:

> Our father in heaven Hallowed by Thy name. Thy kingdom come Thy will be done on earth, as it is in heaven. Forgive us our sins as we forgive, those who

forgive against us. Lead us not into temptation, for the power and the glory are yours ever and for ever. (Lk: 11, 1-4).

Yes, we cannot but utter an 'Amen' at the unforeseen suffering showered on us in dispensing our duty. Every good duty is salvific, apostolic and it ought to be accomplished. The other divine in Monsignor Quixote exposes that doubt can be the source of suffering. Father Quixote, who finds his faithful Sancho in the deposed Marxist Mayor of El Tobaso, shares his doubt with him. But in the course of their travels and arguments both were trying vie the other with each one's respective faith. But they discover that "Its human to doubt"[30] and reveals "how sharing a sense of doubt can bring men together perhaps ever more than sharing a faith" (MQ 59). But when Guardia of Osera violently kills father Quixote the Sancho brings out his or rather their plight. "It is only human to doubt, father Quixote had told him, but to doubt, he thought, is to lose the freedom of action. Doubting, one, begins to waver between one action and another" (MQ 255). But the Mayor's love for father transcends unwaveringly "in spite of the final separation and final silence".

It is in this gap filling between the spiritual and the physical and transcending the limitations imposed by individual and social consciousness that Graham Greene finds the tangible and the intangible, physical and metaphysical as a complement in *Contrast*. The Marxist mayor and father Quixote is a contrast in a metaphysical realm to transcend the doubt of life in love. This attempt to put up a transcendent pattern on evil and on the stifling influence on human psyche is in Scobie's fall, in Pinkie's fall in Raven's lament on the lack of sufficient reason other than oneself to trust, and in Andrew's emptiness. In the deliberate adherence to an infallible Catholic Church for the frame of matured novel,

Graham Greene finds an earthy abode of love that absolves all perversions and takes us to in the possibility of sublimation. The practical mode in which the church appears differs according to the puzzling complexity of life. Intense involvement in human affairs causes suffering and the gravity of suffering increases with knowledge.

> . . . Thus in proportion as knowledge attains to distinctness, as consciousness ascends, pain also increases, and reaches its highest degree in man. And then, again, the more distinctly a man knows the more intelligent he is, the more pain he has, the man who is gifted with genius suffers most of all.[31]

The increase of knowledge and the proportionate increase in suffering is explicated by Graham Greene as well as Brian Moore in *A Burnt-out Case* in *The Great Victorian Collection* respectively. The burnt-out butt of life, Querry, relates "self expression is a hard and selfish thing. It eats everything, even the self. At the end you find you haven't even got a self to express. I have no interest in anything, any more, doctor."[32]

This is the loss of faith Dr. Maloney experiences in his effort to keep the accomplishment of his genius intact. Even his mother disbeliefs his dream and calls it a "fake" His wife separates, his university profession is threatened and he falls in sleeplessness and sex and commits suicide.

David Pryce Jones points out that human involvement is a suffering:

> So long as human life is maintained, people will involve themselves in others. The involvement is necessarily a process of suffering, for all of us, priest, Ryckers or Querrys are stupid, selfish and arbitrary.[33]

In this background of genius' loss of a faith at the involvement either of politics or any alien forces the whisky priest compels an assent in the plane of transcendence.

Greene's conversion was the basic fodder of his writing, than the journey, but he openly admitted that there was a catholic novelist whom he appreciated deeply. He refers to Brain Moore as "My favourite living novelist". This great, sincere confession by the novelist of his appreciation of another novelist of the Catholic genre has his biographical background too. Since he too appreciated Marxism at first, and since he did not have much close affinity and affiliations to the Catholic preachments and practice of faith at the very inception of his life when he got converted, his mind might have been on the slippery ground as far as the theological doctrines and devotional practices of the church were concerned. Brian Moore, who was born and brought up and educated as a staunch Catholic - for that matter, he has been accused by critics as having "obsession" with the Catholic Church - might have served as a mirror through which to look at his own works and to asses, appreciate and even to take a deviation to modernize himself Brian Moore might have served as a ground from which to grasp the functioning of the interior unit of the Church.

Brian Moore too depended on the primary data provided by Graham Greene. In his introduction to Black Robe he writes: "A few years ago, in Graham Greene's Collected Essays, I came upon his discussion of The Jesuits in North America, the celebrated work by the American historian Francis Parkman". (BR 2). From there Brian Moore concluded just as Greene concluded after his visit to Liberia, "a voice speaks to us directly from the seventeenth century, the voice of the conscience that, I fear, we no longer possess" (BR 2).

The moral dictum that impels Brian Moore to beckon the voice and the taunting way of alleging England of its indifference, is the same missionary zeal thirsting for Christianity as a panacea to the shattered, broken and butchered part of the world. Greene has seen the dirt, disease, the barbarity and the familiarity of Africa, yet he felt the deep appeal of the seedy. "It is nearer the beginning like

Monrovia, its building was begun wrong, but at least it was only begun, it has not reached so far way as the smart, the new, the ethic, the cerebral." (PG 3)

Both Graham Greene and Brian Moore depict an "outsiders" sense: Greene's *The Man Within*, *England Made Me* and *It is a Bafflefield'* are expostulations of the same thesis. Tim Heald writes:

> Moore is sometimes compared with Graham Greene who apparently much admires him. This comparison is often thought to be something to do with their mutual interest in Catholicism, but I think their outsider's sense of place is most important. They write about communities that are not their communities but which they have studied intimately. In doing so they provide insights denied to the inhabitants.[34]

If Greene appreciates him, it is because the carping meaningless movements of man like a fish out of water in the arena of life at the loss of an anchorage in life, a loss of faith and the effort to substitute an ideal is analysed by him allegorically in his fictions. John Wilson Foster writes "I think it was Greene who said that governing passion lends a unity to any shelf of books."[35]

The governing passion of the two novelists is one in its final analysis: the Catholic faith in its crisis, zest, propagation, life giving aspects and depicting man's normlessness and agonies of aspirations which are lacking a vital faith. Both the novelists thus ratify Elizabeth Bowen's worlds, "A man's whole art may be rendered down, by analysis, to variations upon a single theme.[36]

For convenience's sake Brian Moore's study of Catholic involvement in life can be divided as follows: (1), repressive dimension of faith in action (2) the progressive dimension of faith in action, (3) the ameliorative dimensions of faith in action and (4) the perfective or sublimative dimension of faith. These aspects of faith and its working on the protagonist is the seminal point of suffering in his fictions.

What is unique in Brian Moore is that he knows the internal structure of the Catholic Church from the primary unit-the monastic cell and this is dramatically painted in *Catholics*.

Catholics provides faith in action in the internal dimension of the Churches' basic unit - the Monastery. Suffering is the process of surrender and the power and the glory of life is found by the Abbot in obedience and docility. Modernising the monastic ego, the pain it inflicts on persons, the mad adherence and obsession to religious observation and religion belittled to devotionalism and ritualistic observations and a faith that is not large enough for any moment and change of life, the tragedy of stereotype formation and the rigidity that do not give space to aggiornamento; a faith that lacks the lap of luxury and mad fanaticism getting rooted in asceticism, where self imposition is more than obedience to God's will are depicted here in abundant tension in the fisherman's parabolic setting, leaving us to a rejuvenated, reinterpreted, reformative acceptance of the first vow and the arduous execution of it even in the moment of great peridition - the personal loss of faith. In freedom, determination gets meaning and fate is defeated. In *The Power and the Glory* the priest lost this self in all aspects, morally, physically and even in material wealth but even then he kept his self-image in executing the decision of his will to be loyal to Jesus in administering the scared bread. Faith in keeping human will power is never subdued except to God, its creator. The monk and the priest, are modern men caught up, in the whirlpool of crisis, and schizophrenic deviants for their faith. J. O'Donoghue writes:

> Moore's most consistent concern in his thirty years of writing novels has been belief or faith in its widest sense and that this is the theme that gives his work both coherence and significance.[37]

Brian Moore confesses:

> I have always been interested in the fact that people must believe in something – nuclear disarmament, love as a regenerating force, politics, anything. When I discuss belief I discuss it as a question of what stops us from the accidie of despair, of saying we're only here to reproduce our species.[38]

Then later in Moore's work religious faith is seen as a form of belief:

> I found, when I started to write, I became very interested in the question of faith . . . . The virtue of having a belief in something. I began to see and feel, as I do now, that the great lack of modern life is the lack of a belief in something greater than ourselves.[39]

Belief can mean anything an individual holds dear, an ideal, an inspiration, a goal, but it can also mean a religious belief. Moore has not always perceived institutional religion and Catholicism as a valid focus of belief; Graham Greene disliked the designation "Catholic Novelist", but his hostility to religion and Catholicism in particular has gradually disappeared and he now sees spiritual faith not just as another kind of belief but as the highest kind there is. In his The search for the self O' Donghue writes:

> After 1960, and after two Belfast novels, Moore's writings entered a phase which lasted until the late 1970s and which therefore encompasses the majority of his works. The novels of 1960s and 1970s, in general, are pre-occupied with the individuals search for self fulfilment . . . . The Revolution script was published in 1971 and Catholics, which followed in 1972.[40]

Catholics is more serious and more problematic. It does concern itself with belief and in one sense, despite the focus on organized religion is affirmed by its title that it treats belief as a secular issue. The conflict at the centre of the novel is two-fold: between two different visions of how the Church mediate faith in a secular world and between the different forms of belief by James Kinsella and Thomas O'Malley. Kinsella, according to the new dispensation believes in a secularised version of Catholicism, while the skeptical Abbot, though presiding over the most ritualised and spiritual form of Catholicism surviving in the new world is inwardly conscious that his real role is a secular one of a foreman or manager of the monastery. However, the clerical protagonists in Catholics make it significantly different from those novels with secular characters which address the issue of secular belief. Donoghue remarks:

> The heightened style, the portentous symbols, the ritualistic simplicity of confrontation, the lack of depth in the treatment of opposing beliefs interesting, though the protagonists show the uneasiness of Moore with his subject.[41]

In *The Power and The Glory* the guardian of a secular city is pitted against the hound of heaven or the champion of the "celestial city" to bring about the tension of the novel so as to absorb the mind of the peruser into it; whereas in Catholics, Brian Moore employs the peripheral secular attitude of an ecclesiastical plenipotentiary. The general's delegate's complaint against the church, is a popularly alleged one by the Protestants- the private confession and old mass. It is now contrasted against an apparently conservative attitude of the Abbot. Thus faith in its secular faces is brought out with all its suffering and tension culminating, ultimately, in the surrender of "the will".

The one who read Graham Greene requires another set of mind for Catholics. For, to defamiliarise the structure of the travelogue, which is a common metaphor of our life, Brian Moore uses an entirely different beginning. In the former a hunted apostle who deeply feels the loss of "the salt" in him travels through a riped wineyard – a flock of lost men under the Marxist regime and aspiring for a "nearer the beginning". Like a Melchisedech, the priest, through the chilling atmosphere, meets Tench and many who needed his care and confront a betrayal by a Mestigo in the figure of Judas, gets imprisoned and then subjects him to a shot and replaces "Lord, why you have forsaken me" of Jesus Christ by "Hail, Christ the king".

For another "aggiornamento" in the internal dimension of primary unit of the Church - "microcosm" of the world - Brian Moore brings in a modern priest with an index book in hand and a message to set in modernisation.

> In the fog lifted air, looking at the pier, the visitor walked to the disused pier. In that morning light he thought of Rome. In the Lungotevere Vaticano, he had been handed an out of print book: *Weirs Guide to Religious Monuments*.[42]

Then we are led into the history of the Monastery as it is recorded.

Muck Abbey, Kerry, Ireland, on a small island off the rocky panoramic coastline of the Atlantic ocean is known as 'The Ring of Kerry'. The Monastery (Albanesian order), founded 1216, rebuilt between 1400-70, has a cell on the mainland, the priory of Holy Cross at Mount Coom near the village of Cahirciveen.

> . . . This priory, sacked by Cromwellian troops, was in penal times, a place for clandestine mass, conducted in the open air on a "mass rock" altar. The abbey itself (on Muck Island) escaped from Wellian despoliation and sits on the western slope of the Island overlooking a splendour of sea (C 7).

With this description our imagination is brought to the realistic realm. Again our imagination gets challenged to go forward in the next line "From the Abbey tower the visitor looks down on grey-waves which court on barren rock. The monks, fish and gather kelp" (C 7).

Thus the fishermen are introduced as in the Bible. Then the gulls in search of fish, the boat and sheds and the promise of a boat by the "padraiz" and he himself coming along shortly to accompany and how the monks use to drive to Cahir Civeen on a Sunday - some 20 miles distance and how they stop singing mass if the sea is rough, all bring out the dedication and care by which they led the flock forward.

Just as the priest in *The Power and the Glory*, Briar Moore's priest Kinsella too mixes himself with a hotelier and gets the information that the Island boat will not land without the Abbot's permission and even confession itself is controlled by putting up a sign saying "parishners only for confession", the priest delegate from Rome gets the pulse of the place. Thus he gathers data about how the monk still sticks to private confession. Public confession where the whole congregation stands before mass and says an act of contrition, according to Kinsella, took place everywhere else.

Thus the internal tension of the novel is introduced. Then again parallel to the ignominy to which the priest in *The Power and the Glory* is subjected, in *Catholic*, the "plenipotentiary" is also subjected to jealousy by Catholic Pentecostals. In Herons Hotel "the girl was out and after a time, when she realised it was Fr. Kinsella, she agreed. That Fr. James Kinsella had booked and it was arranged" (C 12). Her reiterated call as 'Father', 'Father' elicited scorn from the Catholic Pentecostals and his towards them as he went to the Stairs" (C 13).

The difference with which "Visher" – (the friend of James) fills Jim (James K) takes the reader to a serious tone of the book:

> People are sheep. they haven't changed they want their old parish priests and those old family doctors. Sheep

> needs authoritarian sheep dogs nipping at their heels from birth to funeral People don't want truth or social justice. They don't want ecumenical tolerance. They want certainties. The old parish priest promised that, you can't Jim. (C 13)

Suddenly, our mind is taken back to the sound of the boat pulsing, coming, carrying the painful confrontation. To bring home the reader to the bone of contention the author still makes us await by repeating what Fr. General said at the inception of the journey. "This will not be your first visit to Ireland" (C 14) and bringing his Harward and Yeatsian school background so as to present us with Kinsella's new and rich background.

As a sharp contrast to this we are told of the background of "The recalcitrant Abbot of Muck" as it was given by the General.

> He is one Thomas O'Malley now in the sixty-ninth year. The son of Greengocer. The Abbot is the product of the Irish seminary, of course a prize winner in Latin and served in Balkmoore Abey in Kent then Ireland, Dublin . . . Muck. Cast down on some Island and abandoned at an early age . . . order had no great hopes of him. The thirty monks of fishermen living in an income from kelp . . . all the General gets from an old chapter house record book . . . Xerox sheet, microfilmed. (C 14-15)

From there we are led to the history of the abbey which was begun at the behest of Saint Patrick – Irish Saint by local king, there is no priory now. These are nearly parishes, the monks cross to the mainland to say mass and sacerdotal duties. All suggestions of the Irish provincials are not headed by Abbot. So the General asks him: "Get the old fool down off that mountain, sane. If he gives you any trouble, bite him" (C 17).

Thus, we have Kinsella with all the fodder provided with for a confrontation. Through a contrast in background, and characters; of the two members of the same monastery, our curiosity is elicited. Thus once the veterans' are arrayed with their peculiar background, in the diesel-engined tentonner with his 'despatch case', Kinsella starts.

To relieve the reader of the tiresome journey and matter-of-fact narration, Brian Moore skilfully fuses in between to get the reader in harmony with nature. But there too Brian Moore keeps the religious atmosphere in the description of nature. "Rainbow arched, raindrops came down, thunder clouds began to take possession of the sky. He felt cold. He thought of Hartmann in the rain forests of Brazil (C 24). In a superb master-stroke Brian Moore excels all others when he writes:

> The rainbow seemed to end in the centre of the white cross formed by two concrete ribbons of road. The onomatopoeic device? Two roads, the rainbow ending and in the centre a white cross, all suggestive of the coming multifaceted dazzling splendour of the two in their confrontation. (C 24)

The conversation begins in a peaceful note but mounts on in tension not only between the two veterans, but among the whole community. When Martin led Kinsella the Abbot apologises 'I am sorry that you were left alone to stand on the pier by padraig. "You brought the symbol of the Century you brought the first flying machine to Muck" (C 29). "I have a letter for you from father General. And this is my ecumenical order of Mission (C 29) is the response of Kinsella.

To elicit the reader's response there is a beautiful description, "The Abbot's hands were a workman's and had rough boots. When he read the general's letter, he thought that the Abbot had a power, a presence, which recalled the Italian painting (C 34). Forty years have lapsed since he held General's letter and he exclaimed spontaneously he acclaimed

"A red letter day". The tragic rejection of the Abbot by the General creates a sympathy in the mind of the peruser adding to the dynamic superiority of the reader. The Abbot says "This type of place in Ireland is known as the Back of Beyond. You are now in the Back of Beyond" (C 35). But the Abbot recalls that in Christendom there is no back of beyond, and even Pope Pious the Second asked the Abbot Walter Tabor to teach the dean of Kerry.

The historical incident of Hartman's banishment when he disobeyed the Bishop and the villagers refused him food and the Abbot's self-reflection "what could I do in this forsaken spot" all make the reader come to grips with the gravity of the situation.

The discord that exists on the theological side of the sacraments of Eucharist and confession is the central theme of the novel Fr. Manus Fr. Mathew, Fr. Walter and the 28 monks are for the retention of the old Mass, confession and prayer. According to Manus "This new mass is not a mystery. It's a mockery – a sing-song. It is not talking to God, it is talking to your neighbour, that is why it is in people's language of any country" (C 47). The grace they say at supper too is not the approved ecumenical grace. When Kinsella feels that for this too they are adamant in their old ones, he remarks that he is not an inquisitor, "we are trying to introduce a uniform posture" (C 60). But the Abbot defends his inflexible mind by saying that the old one is practised not to destroy the faith of congregation who comes for mass.

The Abbot frowns on the issue of private confession "All mortal sins are mortal to the soul. I find these new rulings difficult to apply" (C 63). But Kinsella opposes and calls private confession "a serious mistake". When he opines that this private confession is distasteful to other ecumenical groups and now the easier from has been sanctioned by Vatican, the Abbot retorts: "I am not concerned with V or IV, but I am limited to this parish. We do not want to disturb the faith of the people" (C 65). The Abbot is greatly afraid of getting the label of a counter revolutionary and acting against Vatican. He condemns the TV which publicises all. Programmes in wrong hands about this subject could be made to look like the first strings of a Catholic Counter revolution (C 65). When Kinsella accuses the Abbot of contradicting Vatican IV, the Abbot emotionally responds: "I did not think of myself as contradicting Rome. God forbid" (C 68).

At last the Abbot reverses the coin saying: "I have been a priest for 40 years. But when a young fellow like you kneels down in Church, do you pray? Do you actually say prayers like 'Our Father, Hail Mary'. What is Mass to you" (C 67). Kinsella is thus compelled to expose the secular tenor of his faith thus: I do not believe that the wine and bread is changed into body and blood except in a purely symbolic manner. I do not in the old sense, think of God as actually being present in the tabernacle (C 67).

The Abbot ludicrously laughs at the folly of the champion of the infallible Church saying:" yet you seem to be what I would call a very dedicated young man" (C 67). After assessing the standard belief of this day and age that is reflected in the young priest, the Abbot challenges him for punishment. Here dawns the great experience which the receptionist critic Stanley Fish advocates in a good text. It is a superb moment when the reader feels really superior getting enlightened in comprehension. The irony becomes obvious when a young priest who has no deep foundation in faith is asked to punish an Abbot who served the Lord for more than forty years as a priest. The Abbot remarks: "As a plenipotentiary you can take punishment. The letter made it clear I must be gluten for punishment" (C 68). Here Brian Moore is providing us with a contrast in the lieutenant of the Institutional Church (as it is in the case of the lieutenant who stands for Marxism in the Power and the Glory) and the subjective innocent faith of the Abbot to enable our sincerity to defend real faith.

The decision to sit together to think of the general's letter, the ring from Dinsle and the warning of the storms at noon take us both to the external world as well as to the internal monastery. For when the guest room is unlocked, after his sleep, Kinsella has already reached the solution "Obedience is the trump card. Tu as Partis. And on this rock I will build my Church and the gates of hell will not prevail against you" (C 73). But then he hears a din of music. There is none to be seen. He finds that rules are broken. None of the monks are in bed. He finds that Fr. Walter and Fr. Manus assumed the role of ringleaders making the monks to pray against a renovation either in Eucharist or any of the sacraments or prayer. In a most poignant mood of a loss of identity, the Abbot is wildly showing them to disperse to their cells:" if I cannot trust you to carry out an order, then where am I?" (C 78). He calls himself "prelates nullius"-nobody's prelate. This sense of the loss of self identity in a Senior Abbot is so powerfully described that we are spontaneously involved in the situation both emotionally and intellectually. Moore writes: "To night he sat in the Church, as a man sits in an empty waiting room" (C 79). Again he hears footsteps in the nave. Fr. Mathew, the biggest man of the Muck, the novice master is now calling others: "where are the others. It is time to vigil to preserve the Latin Mass on Mount Coom and here on Muck" (C 81). At last to quell Fr. Mathew the Abbot has recourse to the vow of obedience: When you were ordained as an Albanesian Monk, you made a Solemn promise to God to obey your Superiors. Go to bed (C 81).

This is a moment of mounting tension. A long time friend and a member of the monastic family has to be scorned and scoffed at midnight. The Abbot has to face horizontal and vertical beams of suffering in executing the orders from Rome and in Confronting the opposition both from his conscience and from his inmates. Thus the novel illustrates prophetically what has befallen to the Catholic monastic life after the Second Vatican Council. As Second Vatican Council stated, it was just an opening of the windows of the Church. But conservatives and liberalists have turned many holy places, where 'angels fear to tread' to scenes of pandemonium.

In the first chapter itself Brian Moore defamiliarises Kinsella from other missionaries by depicting a unique type of journey, *In Black Robe*, Fr. Laforgue's journey is with a group of Algonkian Indians and for the purpose of mission work among the Canadian Indians. In *The Colour of Blood* Cardinal Bem is an authority fighting against those groups of Bishops and spys supporting them. But there too the political trap is familiar to us. In Cold Heaven the journey is a pleasure trip and follows the accident. Dr. Maloney's journey is for academic purpose. Bernard and Mona in *The Temptation of Eileen Hughe's* share a business and familiar atmosphere of the family and attention is sought on the shifting of the journeys. But in *Catholics* a theological unit that has taken its origin in the words of Jesus Christ "I shall make you fishers of man" serves the cause of the journey. Thus in the parabolic net of fishermen we are caught up by the new apostolic delegate of the Superior General who arrives by an aeroplane to collect information and to correct the code of monks who are fighting the odds of life both in an outside sea. This contrast and defamiliarising technique create gap in our mind granting space to ponder over. It is in this gap that we meet the conversation between the Abbot and Kinsella, even the core sacrament of faith the Eucharist – in a secular mood, and we are ludicrously involved in the scene. This conversational confrontation makes the faithful to examine their personal stand on the matter of the articles of faith.

An abbot and the young delegate who have dedicated themselves in a solemn vow on the altar of the Lord are now, finding themselves on a secular footing. The Abbot concludes in a desperate mood that he is a "mere foreman of fishermen" in "the back of the beyond" of the region – Island diplomatically reveals his lack of strong faith in prayer. But even in this aridity, a surrender is what is required. But all monastery is divided when the Abbot surrenders in the act of prayer in obeying the General. we find the supreme moment of faith in action, sought after by Graham Greene throughout his literary career. Action for mere living limits the suffering to periphery but action in faith involves the mind as well as the soul.

The shape of this theological kingdom is the shape of the novel. Jurisdictional higher authority from Rome with a duty comes to a remote monastery to set right the liturgy and sacraments not only shapes our imagination but enlighten our brain through a new light, through the functioning of hierarchical Church, its internal machinery, the sentiments, and belief of the followers and the dedication required of the churchmen. The strong chord of the Church and its fabric in a theological symbol make the Church akin to contemporary men and challenge to think and get transformed in terms of faith.

Thus as in Graham Greene, here too the pattern or the gestalt – is a symmetrical search which takes us back to the command of Jesus, "seek and thou shall find' – conformity and surrender finds the culmination of human cognition in faith. The tension of the tussle of the Church leaders makes the novel the "terrain of tension".

In *The Power and the Glory* the whisky priest is placed against a communist lieutenant and the fight of two will, two forces, the secular and the religious and in proclaiming 'Hail Christ the King' at the moment of death, in self-sacrifice. Graham Greene proves that The Power and the Glory of God is still alive in the distorted, disrupted and disordered phase of the world; Kinsella represents the power of God and the surrender of Abbot is the glory of God on earth.

When the Abbot kneels down in the chapel and praying "our father in Heaven . . . . he too ends his prayer for the power and the glory are yours. The terror terrain of *The Power and the Glory* ends in surrender of life and the tension terrain of the *Catholics* ends in "surrender of will, ego", both by divines, and is the answer for our "the search for faith in action". What was left as an open Gestalt by Graham Greene in *The Man Within*, *England Made Me* and *It's a Battlefield* is complemented by Brain Moore in *Catholics* through the primary unit of the liturgical theological life of the monastery. It is the answer to the muddled internal life and a formless world of battlefield either for money or dominance rendered in the dynamic suffering surrender to God. To elicit the insight into the elements and processes of suffering in the individual ego, both Graham Greene and Brain Moore delve deeply into the individual consciousness from opposing poles of existence. In *Rose and Pinkie* the ethical and the metaphysical dimensions are contrasted. The whisky priest is contrasted with the Marxist Lieutenant, and the physical and theological realms are contrasted in the personal life of the priest. Monsignor Quixote's Sancho is a Marxist Mayor and Querry's escape from the city life is to a "graceless chumming world." Parallel to this, Brian Moore's protagonists are groping in their search in a Catholic society, in the first novels like, *The Lonely Passion of Judith Hearne*, *An Answer from Limbo*, *I am Mary Dunne*. In *The Emperor of Ice-cream* the warring purposeless world of adults increases the poignancy of the protagonist. But the protagonists of *Black Robe*. *The Colour of Blood* and Dhillon in *The Lies of Silence* suffer the pain inflicted on them by angst for the loss of souls. It may be a loss felt in for the soul of *Catholics* under a Marxist regime; or as Dhillon looks at it, it may be due to the lies that keep people in a morbid state by the parliaments and pulpits that do not shake us from the life of a contented complacency. The IRA and Dillon present the contrast.

These contrasting phenomena in these novelists create gaps in the readers' mind and ultimately challenge them to a metaphysical jump, to an intuition, to a realization, that a transcendent pattern, a belief either in God or in a secular cause like politics is required to pull on as the Sons of God.

It seems that these novelists agree with W.H. Clark: "Some form of stimulation to produce unease and restlessness is necessary for any kind of growth and learning."[43] The evils and abnormalities that make the protagonists of these novelists, losers, are significant from the point of view of search. For William James remarks:

> The evil facts which refuses positively to account for are a genuine portion of reality; and they after all be the best keys to life's significance, and positively the only openers of our eyes to the deepest levels of truth.[44]

What Kierkegaard calls "Sickness unto death" is the indispensable factor of a believing world. So the Catholic novelists who are explicating the involvement of human being in the background of Catholicism cannot but deal with suffering. For the protagonist's life is a living in faith. For in two of the best known chapters of *The Varieties of Religious Experience* written by William James, "The Religion of Healthy Mindedness, and "The Sick Soul", James describes two different expression of religious sentiment: Doubt and conflict, for example, are much more associated with the "sick soul", the individual for whom religion and life itself will mean suffering. Of course it will be difficult to find the completely sick soul or the completely healthy minded. Each individual is a blend of the two"[45]

The "heart-piercing", "reason-bewildering" world of Graham Greene's and Brian Moore's fictions compels us to the transcendental, theological conclusion of Cardinal

Newman.

> To consider the world in its length and breadth, its various history, the many races of man, their starts, their fortunes, their mutual attention, their conflicts, and their ways, habits, government, forms of worship, their enterprise, their aimless courses, . . . mental anguish, the prevalence and intensity of Sin, the pervading idolatries, the corruptions, the dreamy hopeless irreligion, that conditions the whole race, so fearfully yet exactly described in Apostles words 'having no hope and without God in the world – all this is a vision to dizzy and appall, and inflicts upon the mind the sense of profound mystery, which is absolutely beyond human solution. What shall be said to this heart-piercing, reason bewildering fact, I can only answer that either there is no creator, or this living society of men in a true sense discarded from His presence . . . if there be a God, since there is a God, the human race is implicated in some terrible aboriginal calamity" (LR XVIII).

NOTES

1. Will Durant, *The Story of Philosophy* (New York: Washington Square, 1961) 323.
2. Ibid, 326.
3. *Holy Bible*, Matthew 10:38.
4. M. Macneil Dixon, *The Human Situation* (Harmondsworth: Penguin, 1937) 82.
5. Alfred Adler, *Guidance and Counselling: Principles and Techniques* (M.Ed Notes, Madurai Kamaraj University Package 1-2, 1989) 35.
6. Ibid, 35.
7. Graham Greene, *Our Man in Havana* (1958, Harmondsworth: Penguin, 1971) 190-90.
8. Graham Greene, *The Honorary Consul* (1971, Harmondsworth: Penguin, 1975) 1. Further references to this edition will be indicated in the text by the abbreviation HC followed by page number.

9. Graham Greene, *The Quiet American* (195, Harmondsworth: Penguin 1977) 87-88.
10. Brian Moore, *The Temptations of Eileen Hughes* (London: Cape, 1981) 159. Further references to this edition will be indicated in the text by the abbreviation TEH followed by page number.
11. Graham Greene, *Brighton Rock* (1938, Harmondsworth: Penguin, 1977) 226. Further references to this edition will be indicated in the text by the abbreviation BR followed by page number.
12. Graham Greene, *The Man Within* (1929, Harmondsworth: Penguin, 1977) 24. Further references to this edition will be indicated in the text by the abbreviation MW followed by page number.
13. Graham Greene, *A Gun for Sale*, (1936; Harmondsworth: Penguin, 1975) Further references to this edition will be indicated in the text by the abbreviation GS followed by page number.
14. Graham Greene, *The Ministry of Fear* (1993; Harmondsworth: Penguin, 1976), 165.
15. Graham Greene, *The Third Man* (1950: Harmondsworth: Penguin, 1976). 106.
16. Graham Greene, *It's a Battlefield* (1934; Harmondsworth: Penguin, 1977) 28.
17. Graham Greene, *The Heart of the Matter* (1948; Harmondsworth: Penguin, 1977) 157. Further references to this edition will be indicated in the text by the abbreviation HM followed by page number.
18. Brian Moore, *The Lonely Passion of Judith Hearne* (Boston: Little Brown, 1956) 19. Further references to this edition will be indicated in the text by the abbreviation JH followed by page number.
19. Brian Moore, *The Feast of Lupercal.* (London: Andre Deutsch, 1950) 15. Further references to this edition will be indicated in the text by the abbreviation FL followed by page number.
20. Brian Moore, *The Lies of Silence* (London: Bloomsbury, 1990) 49. Further references to this edition will be indicated in the text by the abbreviation LS followed by page number.
21. Brian Moore, *The Great Victorian Collection* (London: Cape, 1975) 25. Further references to this edition will be indicated in the text by the abbreviation GVC followed by page number.
22. Brian Moore, *I am Mary Dunne* (London: Cape, 1968) 25. Further

references to this edition will be indicated in the text by the abbreviation MD followed by page number.

23. Brian Moore, *An Answer from Limbo* (London: Andre Deutsch, 1963) 10. Further references to this edition will be indicated in the text by the abbreviation AL followed by page number.
24. Brian Moore, *The Colour of Blood* (London: Cape, 1985) 2. Further references to this edition will be indicated in the text by the abbreviation CB followed by page number.
25. Graham Greene, *The Power and the Glory* (1943; Harmondsworth: Penguin, 1967) 6. Further references to this edition will be indicated in the text by the abbreviation PG followed by page number.
26. Graham Greene, *The Lawless Roads* (1939; Harmondsworth: Penguin, 13. 1976) 13. Further references to this edition will be indicated in the text by the abbreviation LR followed by page number.
27. Herman S. Schwartz, *The Art of Relaxation*, (Bombay: Jaico, 1991) 33.
28. VS Seturaman, 177.
29. Louis Evely, *Suffering* (London: Burns and Oates, 1968) 59.
30. Graham Greene, *Monsignor Quixote* (1982; Harmondsworth: Penguin, 1983) 58. Further references to this edition will be indicated in the text by the abbreviation MQ followed by page number.
31. Durant, *op. cit.*, 325.
32. Graham Greene, *A Burnt Out Case* (1961, Harmondsworth: Penguin, 1977) 46. Further references to this edition will be indicated in the text by the abbreviation BOC followed by page number.
33. David Pryce-Jones, *Graham Greene* (London: Oliver and Body, 1963) 96.
34. Tim Heald, "The Wearing of the Gene" in Books in Canada 8:8 (1979) 11-13 qtd in *Contemporary Literary Criticism*, 19, 333.
35. John Wilson Foster, 'Question and Answer with Brian Moore', (Irish Literary Supplement) 4, 1985) 6.
36. Robert Macauley and George Lanning, *Technique in Fiction*, (New York: Harper and ROW, 1964) 6.
37. J. O'Donoghue, *Brian Moore: A Critical Study* (Montreal: McGill-Queen's UP, 1991) XV.

38. Ibid, XV.
39. Ibid, XV.
40. Ibid, 67.
41. Ibid, 68.
42. Brian Moore, *Catholics* (London: Cape, 1972) 7. Further references to this edition will be indicated in the text by the abbreviation with C followed by page number.
43. W.H. Clark, *The Psychology of Religion* (New York: Macmillan, 1959) 170.
44. William James, *The Varieties of Religious Experience*. (London: Longman, 1952) 160.
45. Ibid, 154-155.

3 ART AS AGAPE

Man's search for humanity is superbly endeavoured in fictions. In this deliberate dwelling on life and how justice, mercy and love in the process of life cement human interaction, the attention of the writer should be fixed above the confines of the limited predicaments of man's mundane existence. In this conscious attempt the genius, whether creative or constructive, has to purge his writing soul and take a detached disposition that is rooted in the communion of the universals. This communion and the artistic transference of it in life demand a self sacrificing love. This is clearly stated by T.S. Eliot when he writes:

> The progress of the artist is a continued self-sacrifice, a continual extinction of personality. It is in this process of depersonalisation that art may be said to approach to the condition of science.[1]

To avoid the possible misconception that art is for emotional escape, T.S. Eliot further states.

> "The emotion of art is impersonal, and the post cannot reach this impersonality without surrendering himself wholly to the work to be done."[2]

Graham Greene's Querry in *A Burnt-cut Case* and Brian Moore's Anthony Maloney in *The Great Victorian Collection* are typical illustrations of modern artists, who are surrounded by "belief, half-belief and non-belief". The ennui that they face and the stiff resistance from the rigid stereotyped expectations of society are a study in complement, leading us to the discovery of the self-loosening and the entangling factors that stunt the life of a creative artist.

According to St. Augustine the theological uniformity of all artistic endeavour is to be found in the *Book of Genesis*:

> Man is created in the likeness of God. This likeness begins now to be formed again in us. It is not surprising that even in life a man would be represented like thus, not as he is, but as he ought to be impossibly, Superior to the accidents of temporal manifestation.[3]

When it is said that "man does not live by bread alone but by every word that proceedeth out of the mouth of God" (Matt IV:4), the *Bible* evinces that a need or "indigence" as Plato calls it, is the first cause of the production of art. Man is a spiritual as well as a psychological being. Man as the reasoning and the mortal animal can live by "bread alone". But "bread alone" is the same thing as merely functional art. But the whole man is what is meant by Jesus. The "words of God" are precisely those ideas and principles that can be expressed whether verbally or visually by art. "The words are visual forms in which they are expressed not merely sensible but significant."[4]

Culture originates in work not in play and activity consists in either a making or a doing. Both of these aspects of the active life depend for their correction upon the contemplative life. "The making of things is governed by art and doing of things by prudence."[5] The importance and universality of art is emphatically asserted:

> . . . every man who is not an artist in some field, everyman without a vocation is an idler . . . . The artist works by art and willingly. The qualities that are required of an artist is beautifully described. . . . It is essential to him or a man to have a right will, and so to have avoided mortal sin.[6]

This classical deliberations on the importance of art and the qualities the artists must have, provide us with a yardstick to count on the protagonists of Graham Greene's and Brian Moore's novels, to evaluate the modern artistic longing in any society. An analysis of Graham Greene's and Brian Moore's artistic protagonists evince how modern culture deprives man of his search for beauty. Beauty is the attractive power of perfection. But the artistic protagonists of Graham Greene and Brian Moore verify the great observation that "It is this way of life (life of perfection) that our civilization denies to the vast majority of men, and in this respect that it is notably inferior to even the most primitive or savage societies with which it can be contrasted."[7]

Though as Graham Greene says in the dedicatory note on *A Burnt-Out Case*, it is an "attempt to give dramatic expression to various types of belief, half-belief, and non-belief" (BOC 48). It presents us with a panoply or rather a panoptic view of modern life through the interactions of different personages in the chromium world.

The critical principle of Wolfgang Iser states that the principle of reverse can be observed at all different levels of the novel:

> Most obviously on the level of the story, and most diffusely in the interplay of characters. . . . First there is the reference to a socially differentiated public that has varying degrees of familiarity with the oppressed poles of town and country. Second, this method of revealing human nature implies a scheme that will determine the structure of the contrast within the story.[8]

In *A Burnt-Out Case* the socially differentiated public in the opposed poles of town and country is portrayed in the personalities of the "graceless chromium world".

Far away from the ruses and intriguing stratagems of a political world, the leprosaria in Belgian Congo, is crowded with a motley collection of people very very "far away from the madding crowd". The "graceless chromium world", - with certain certainties of convictions and a mines of problems of the sickly, theological and secular world - is a forlorn land that satiates and transforms the burnt-out soul. Hopeless sickness and the tremendous optimism of theology and secularism, and rationalistic atheism are all sumptuously banqueted on the table of charity, in a remote land.

What is singular in the "graceless chromium world" is that it is peopled with divines and bon-believers alike. There is a conscientious doctor who is dedicated to see the bright horizon that lies beyond leprosy. Absorbed in "skin tests" and "mutilation cases", the doctor is a beacon of relief for those who are scathed by the dreadful malignant evil. The priests, an unsatisfactory lot, indulging in profane matters of building, finance and practical affairs, are in the general atmosphere of love and charity. But they too share the burnt-out aspects of life in their privacy. The cheroot-smoking superior is a pragmatic man. Father Jean, "carefully nurtured the character of a film-fan, as though it would help him to wipe out an ugly part." (BOC 83). Father Thomas who thinks "for a good man, fame is always a problem" is afraid of the dark because "prayers were of no avail to heal the darkness" (BOC 88). These ecclesiastical dignitaries are contrasted to Doctor Colin who has no faith but faith in the progress of man and a courage of conviction, though an atheist at the root.

To this patch of land of belief and disbelief, Querry the man is fetched in by the boat. He does not know who he is? Where he is going? And the basic question of where are we here? is pondered through him by the author. A disgusted, disgruntled and completely alienated Querry parries all questions about his future. For he has no plans: "I assure you there's nothing of interest in my case. I have retired that's all (BOC 28-29). Existential anguish and nausea scarred the very marrow of his morale of life that he "wants nothing" because he has come to "the end of everything" (BOC 10). His destination in life is brought out when he answers to Dr. Colins' query whether he is going to stop here: "The boat goes no further" (BOC 20). His mind as it is unraveled to the superior is: "I suffer from nothing, I no longer know what suffering is. I have come to the end of that too" (BOC 10).

Like all the rest he too comes to the end of everything. Yes, Querry is a gone with the wind and chance brought him to the "continent of misery and heat". As the epigraph to *The End of the Affair* suggests this morbid state of mind may be to "get open the cells of heart that is not yet open". "It occurred to the doctor that perhaps here too was a man under obedience, but not to any divine or civil authority, only to whatever wind might blow" (BOC 29).

The ego with which he steps into the place is smeared with egotic self-regards, where gloom and despair is pervading:

> The laughter of the clergy irritated him. He was vexed by the pleasure which they took in small matters. The passenger wondered when it was that he had first begun to detest laughter like a bad smell; to his own region where laughter was like the unknown syllables of an enemy tongue (BOC 8).

Querry has not only a corroded self but also "retired" from his faith. He tells Dr. Colin: "Self-expression is a hard and selfish thing. It eats everything, even the self " (BOC 48).

At times he feels sickened by the word "prayer": "I gave it up long ago" (BOC 45). Dr. Colin rightly calls him "a burnt-out case" - a leper in whom the disease has burnt itself out, meaning, glory and significance of life all, vanished from his life.

But Deo Gratias, his servant whom he rescues from the shallow marsh in the forest flickers in his mind an axis, a gleam of peace in Pendele. But when he is challenged for the complicated things by the Superior who remarks: "People have to grow up. We are called to more complicated things than that" (BOC 76). Querry was one step ahead of the consciousness of the complexity of life:

> We've grown up rather badly. The complications have become too complex – we should have stopped with the amoeba – no long before that with the silicates. If your god wanted an adult world he should have given us an adult brain. (BOC 46)

His musings with Dr. Colin in reaction to the superior's preachment brings out what he is. Querry thinks that "it's possible for an intelligent man to make his life without a god." (BOC 81) and he follows Dr. Colin by dedicating to the routine of the dispensary. He scorns at the superior's view of 'mercy' and 'love': "Has it he ever known people to kill with love and kill with mercy?" (BOC 82). Thus the flickering fire of charity enlivens his life; but he is opposed to the sacramental faith the priests preach, though he is living in their pasture.

The contrast between the superior's conception of him and Querry's provocative response make us involve in the baptismal creed of this modern soul.

> You try to draw everything into the net of your faith, father, but you can't steal all the virtues. Gentleness is n't Christian, self-sacrifice is not Christian, Charity isn't, remorse isn't. (BOC 76-77)

Thus without sacrament, Querry is a man of mere secular mode of mercy and love. But how different is he now. The one who declared earlier "Human beings are not my country" (BOC 51) and who detested laughing "like a bad smell" now designs the building of the new hospital. This transformation from degage to engagement is the driving force of ego. Other than an ego, no ego, and no "numinosum" sets him to activate, to enforce or to impel into new creativity. When Father Thomas in a creative and salvific venture, of course, to buttress his own faith, talks: "You won't understand how much one needs, sometimes to have one's faith fortified by talking to a man who believes" (BOC 91); Querry protests that he is not a man of faith. When Father Thomas insists" "We both of us have our doubts" (BOC 91) Querry pleads:

> I have long ceased to have doubts. Father, if I must speak plainly, I don't believe at all. Not at all. I've worked it out of my system – like women. I've no desire to convert others to disbelief, or even to worry them. (BOC 91)

But even when Querry completely dispels the path of faith: "If faith were a tree growing at the end of the avenue, I promise you I'd never go that way" (BOC 92), Fr. Thomas counts his disbelief as spiritual aridity and elevates him, a "hero", a "saint in the making". Thus the secular artist is judged divergently by the Churchmen shaking his complacency. This is the environment that he confronts even after his attempt to escape from the intoxicating pain of glory.

An altogether new world is opened to Querry in Rycker-The cauldron of a morsel of past glory and present crisis. Rycker, the ex-seminarian, now a plantation manager counts Querry a holy man, just only to project his theological and sexual frustrations upon him. Faith, for Rycker, is problems: "A faith like ours, when profoundly understood, sets us many problems" (BOC 40) All his words like "prayer", "Contrition", "love of God" are just fodders to excite and entice his wife to gratification of his sex. The glaring egotism and utilitarianism of Rycker's faith as opposed to the secular charitable bent of the artist who flees from the adulations of life without a spiritual anchorage to find a balance, are the superb probe in to the modern architect. In the governor's house Marie get interested in knowing about Querry. "A man of great vision. What he builds lasts. A prayer in stone . . . Mrs. Rycker's had more than mere interest in her old collections: She added the old copy of Time" (BOC 75).

Querry's face covered Lejeune's history. It may lay a discord among the relics of childhood. Then she visits the leproserie with two drums of oil. Her praying in to the details of Querry under the cover of her husband's interest in him at last leads her to ask permission to meet Querry personally.

This visit was a personal need for Querry. The appointment of Parkinson to spiritually blackmail Querry makes Querry active. But Querry has already been printed as "An Architect of Souls", "The Hermit of the Congo" and the thread of a second article "A Saint's past, Redemption by Suffering" made Querry adamant to stop the nonsense.

It seems apparently then the case that Querry, the architect is in search of an inner geography of peace, a pendele, and to get deprive of the befuddling glory of life. He meets Rycker's young and lonely wife whose" "unhappiness was like a hungry animal waiting beside the track for any victim" (BOC 149). Expecting an unwanted child and in the gripping fear of revealing the fact to her husband, that Marie was in need of immediate help, Querry takes Marie to Luc, where she might see a doctor. Querry forgets to tell the bed-ridden Rycker that he is taking Marie out. He does not suspect her a little: "He thought rashly: Poor frightened beast – It was only when they were fully grown you couldn't trust them with your pity" (BOC 149) she stays in the hotel with Querry. At night, Querry tells her a story to send her to sleep. When Parkinson and Rycker follow them to LUC and Rycker on the circumstantial evidence concludes that his wife is carrying "his" – Querry's child, she too admits: "I didn't want him. The only way I could manage was to shut my eyes and think it was you. It was then that the baby must have started." (BOC 149)

From the point of view of contrast there is not much distance between Colin and Querry. When the superior tells God cannot feel disappointment or pain, Colin retorts "Perhaps that's why I don't care to believe in him (BOC 199).

He saw much suffering that goes beyond the might of God to better. The native faith in Nzambi simply aggravates the disease. Colin saw in the lepresorie:

> On the veranda the walking cases' sat out of the sun – if you could call a walking case a man who . . . had to support his huge swollen testicles with both hands. A woman with palsied eyelids . . . A man without fingers nursed a baby in his knees (BOC 46-47)

In such a phase of reality he tells the superior 'your god must feel a bit disappointed, when he looks at this world of his." (BOC 47). And a god who cannot feel a pain or disappointment, he cannot believe in (BOC 47). Colin finds, humanity, the suffering humanity, in his vocation, but no faith; and Querry runs away from vocation for rejuvenation of soul.

Thus the doctor tired of factuality – scorching reality of suffering – views with Sartre the "other as a problem" with no being left to save humanity from the existential torture. Thus the matter in its disharmony and abhorrence make him a professor of "the death of god" to be baptized as an atheist. He is Steeped in indifference, but dedication to the duty makes him organized. Thus in failing to detect the hand of God in human affairs, particularly in suffering as it is revealed through *The Book of Job*, where suffering is revelatory or should be counted as a moment of greater manifestation or epiphany of God, Dr. Colin falls in the lap of disbelief. Unable to find another hand in human affairs he too complements to the normless world of Querry.

In a vivid and vivacious moment Querry unravels his self-image, in one of his long conversation with Colin.

> A writer does not write for his readers, does he? .... The subject of a novel is not the plot He makes buildings (books) in which people can be comfortable, but he is a not interested in their use . . . I have no interest in anything. (BOC 48)

The difficulty in Querry's self-explanation is a mere diagram; he has chosen a self-consuming artists life, perfection of the work is equated to perfection of the office. Even when he is drawn into the service of suffering he protests that "human beings are not my country". For the doctrine of the priests he substitutes, not nature, but a myth of decadence. There is even a secular version of Fr. Thomas's smug theory of aridity in his talk of the artists' regress. Agreeing with Elizabeth Sewell's interpretation that Greene is a novelist of Decadence writing not as catholic but as a neo-Romantic, Kermode writes . . . "Querry more than any other of he heroes is a poseur and ought not to be if the conflict between religious and secular interpretations of his life is to have a valid basis".[9]

This issue becomes very acute in the fairy-tale version of his life which Querry tells Mme Rycker to put her to sleep. Reviewers have called this "embarrassing" yet it is the marrow of the book. It exposes the falsity of Querry's position, not because the stupid priests are necessarily right but because their view of the matter can be fully and ironically presented but this decadent mythology cannot. He speaks of a man who has not been able to detect the hand of God in human life, who sees virtue rewarded by the death of a child (the crucial) test of God in The Heart of the Matter and viciousness punished invisibly. Instead of becoming great artist he becomes a sort of Faberge, making ingenious jewels and enjoying many women. God refuses to allow him to suffer. But although people think he must be very good to have such rewards from God as others who got their legs cut off in accident must be very bad – he finds that, unable to suffer he is unable to love. His jewels are fashionable and people say that he is not only a master technician but deals with serious subject matter because he makes eggs with gold crosses on top "set with precious stones in honour of the king". About this time a mistress committed suicide without his being much disturbed. Then as popular favour waned, the connoisseurs takes him up. At this point the jeweller sees that his work has nothing to do with love, the love of the king for his people, and he wonders as the whole plot of Greens's novel does, whether his unbelief and ugliness of his success are finally proof of the king's existence. While he has been talking the night away the king has in fact been at work in the shape of the prying Parkinson, ensuring that this "success" will amount in the end to the same thing as failure. Only failure can be good, and God is a specialist in Failure. Querry is to have his suffering "with suffering we become part of the Christian myth" (BOC 132). He does not suffer for his own crimes but for those of the Ryckers as in The Heart of the Matter. This is a case of Victimage.

Without belief, Querry, like the artist of his fairy tale is unable to bear success or suffering and without belief Colin is unable to bear the suffering of humanity. This exposes the need of the Lord to bear the fate of life.

God is or should be the anchorage for the equilibrium of mind, for hedonism fails in the case of Querry and humanism of Colin has a fading glory. Therefore the rationale or artistic bent that is suggested is the call of man's life as a vocation to "name the world", as it is illustrated in the *Book of Genesis* by God inviting the first man Adam to name the world as if God has left with no name in his dictionary of the Cosmos, the macrocosm. The mind of these moderns are not rightly organised in this basic call.

This is the theological gestalt to which Querry points to when he replies to Dr. Colin's assertion, "You must have had a lot of belief once to miss it the way you do" (BOC 192). Querry answers:

> I swallowed their myth whole, if you call that a belief . . . ah well, I suppose belief is a kind of vocation and most men haven't room in their brains or hearts for two vocations. If we really believe in something we have no choice, have we, but to go further (BOC 192-193).

Thus a greater conviction in the existential call of man to put his stamp, mark, dominion over the world by imprinting the form which is imbued in him by God through his being fashioned in the "image and likeness" of Him seems to be the gestalt to which the fate of Querry – the disgust of life – the fate of the man; who is trapped in the absurdity of life is pointing to.

The last scuffle of Querry is the absurdity of modern man. As Iser desires, to elicit a response, the book should be a "new vein of knowledge to the modern reader". *A Burnt-out Case* provides this when the self-lost artist gains his last glimpses of glory in the imaginative copulation of Mrs. Rycker with him. But in the ensuing struggle a waterfall of rain suddenly descended on them, Querry made on odd awkward sound which the doctor by now have learned to interpret as a laugh and Rycker fired twice" (BOC 194).

By an adept and dexterous description of the situation Greene makes a most consummate moment of his artistry that will ever be tantalizing but flickers in modern man's secondary imagination: "The lamp fell with Querry and Smashed, the burning wick flared up once under the deluge, lighting an open mouth and pair of surprised eyes and then went out" (BOC 194). Querry confessed that he laughed not at Rycker "I laughed at myself" ".... This is absurd or else...." (BOC 194).

Iser's critical principle states "when the created self of both the author and reader find complete agreement in the text the peruser attains the gestalt and led into comprehension and aesthetic experience"[10]. In *A Burnt Out Case* the author portrays a protagonist whose alienated ego enters into a callous indifference both to glory and pleasure and take route into a road not taken so far – into the leproserie asylum. This flight of the man from the glories of modern life is what the reader experiences in contemporary life situation among the warring demands and normless pleasures of the present social reality. In the purposeless move of Querry the moderns are "teased to think" for an identity and simultaneously compels to "negate the familiar". Thus by negating the familiar the author creates a gap to be filled by the reader and brings in "the superiority in the reader".

Here the principle of contrast too is adroitly used by Graham Greene to effect a reverse to elicit optimum response:

> The contrast that Fielding calls the reverse implies that an idea, a norm or an event can only take on its full shape in the reader if it is accompanied more or less simultaneously by its negative form.[17]

In the company of the scientific doctor and priests whose interpretation are on the lines of spirituality and the Rycker family, who enjoyed life with the collector and Parkinson the news-reporter, the author gives the reader contrasting situations. The doctor's scientific rationality and Querry's stand on life is not strictly contradictory, but contrary. But the interpretation of Querry's life in terms of aridity by priest is untenable. But the reverse takes place absorbing the reader intellectually and emotionally into the text when all the effort to a lease of life is reversed at the end in an irony of contrast in what he avoided. Popularity, a glory and women creep again into his life through the persons of Parkinson and the Ryckers, and Querry casts an absurd laugh on modern life and dies.

Thus the reader is asked to provide link between the beginning and end or the past and present life of Querry and is compelled to conclude upon the irony of contrast in the life of the hero – the protagonist – to realise the absurdity of life. Thus, as is recommended by the reception critic Iser, "the reverse" is obtained both in the plot as well as in the interplay of characters. By depicting the contenting tones in the family life of the Ryckers and the way the child is born, the author makes the novel a story of "bad faith" which is rife in modern world.

If we recapitulate rightly we detect that *A Burnt-Out Case* shades off through allusions and suggestions into an unformulated but nonetheless intended text. It is in this text the reader finds the configurative meaning and experiences the text as a reality. Querry's assessment, that "Self-expression is a hard and selfish thing. It eats everything even the self. At the end you find you haven't even got a self to express" (BOC 48). This is a great artist's realisation and is verified in Anthony Maloney, the central character of Moore's *The Great Victorian Collection*. Querry does not want to be, in terms of Heidegger, "a functional man." Anthony Maloney too does not want to be lost in the history department of the university. But departure from their profession to new phases of life takes quite different pattern. Querry searches for the green pasture of charity and Maloney is caught up in a "secular miracle" challenging him to come out of an egomania. Anthony Maloney's ability to mould reality out of a mere nightmare is in line with Arthur Koestler's conclusion:

> To sum up, it seems to be undeniably true, as Pliny was the first to suggest, that art evolves, like Science in a cumulative manner – but only for a while and within limits, until all that can be done has been done along that particular line, at the great turning points, however, which initiate a new departure along a new line. We find bisociation in the grand style-cross fertilisation between periods, cultures, and provinces of knowledge.[12]

It is this great phenomenon that has taken place in Maloney's artistic invention. For there is nothing to serve as his background. To dream of Victoriana is not given in his background. But his Ph.D. dissertation had been "A study of the effect of Gaining a Coloniel Empire on the Mores of Victorian England as exemplified by the Art and Architecture of the period.[13]

In connection with his work author has been journeying to England to visit museum and libraries and to various public buildings. Thus, while not a recognized expert on Victoriana, he could at least claim a degree of familiarity with the subject. But now this great leap in to a new line compels our curiosity, and is what sounds really original in the setting as well as in the dream.

The protagonist on his way stops in Carmel – a California Coastal resort - which is sometimes described as an "artists' paradise", because he has been told it is a convenient ground from which to explore the Big Sur region. When he has arrived in Carmel and entered the chamber of commerce tourists bureau and enquired about accommodations, a clerk in the bureau recommends the Sea wind.

Dr. Maloney, that ordinary young man is 29 year old and an assistant professor of history at MacGill University in Montreal. It is his first trip to west coast. He has flown out to San Francisco to attempt a seminar at Berkeley. On the last day of the seminar he rents a car and drives south; intending to spend the weekend exploring the Big Sur region. He arrives in Carmel on a Saturday afternoon. On Monday he has to fly home to Montreal. But Maloney does not make his flight. A year later he is still living in Carmel in the same motel room he has checked into on the night of his arrival. A wall has been removed so that the adjoining room can be used as a study. But in essence, his motel bedroom remains unchanged.

There is still some confusion as to when Anthony Maloney first saw the Great Victorian Collection. Can it be said that he first envisaged in his dram? Or did he crate it in its entirety only when he woke up and climbed out of his bedroom window?

Maloney himself is confused after the event. He seems a different person from the ordinary rational young man who had checked into the Sea Winds Motel in Carmel-by-the-Sea, in California on that extraordinary night.

Maloney goes to sleep in a normal manner and passes an uneventful night. Sometime in the early hours of the morning he wakes up, falls asleep again and begins to dream. When he recounts the dream in the television interview the following day, three words appear frequently: "dreamed", "remembered", "recognized". Regarding his dream-twined nightmare he relates:

> I had never seen such a collection. On the opposite aisle to these furnishings I noticed the "Day Dreamer" easy-chair in papier-mâché, decorated at the top with two winged thoughts and made by Jenings and Batteridge; an ivory throne and footstool presented to Queen Victoria by the Rajah of Travancore. . . . Among the larger rooms I recognised the parlor of a famous Victorian brothel and a room containing the furnishings of a Victorian music hall (GVC 8).

This is the realistic picture of the issue of his dream. A deep analysis of the process involved in this night-marish creation of the artifacts reveals that though the unconscious, subconscious and conscious of Dr. Maloney are completely let loose, it is not a religious act, neither is it the outcome of a deep religious experience. For religion is:

> A careful and scrupulous observation of the numinosum . . . that is a dynamic agency or effect not caused by an arbitrary act of the will. . . . The numinosum – whatever its cause may be is an experience of the subject independent of his will. . . .

> The numinosum is either a quality belonging to a visible object or the influence of invisible presence that cause a peculiar alteration of consciousness . . . we might say then that the term "religion" designates the attitude peculiar to a consciousness which has been changed by experience of the "numinosum".[13]

When a man is deprived of this numinosum, he can become obsessed and this leads either to another obsession or mania.

> It is not a matter of indifference whether one calls something a "mania" or a "God". To serve a mania is detestable and undignified but to serve a god is full of meaning and promise because it is an act of submission to a higher, invisible and spiritual being.[14]

Jung regarded the individuating process as a kind of religious process. He thought a religious attitude was natural to man and that modern man was at risk of substituting some inferior kind of worship. When God is not acknowledged, ego mania develops and out of this mania comes sickness. Dr. Maloney is a proven case of the principle; he falls in love with the worship of his own progeny and the whole energy is canalized into a mania and suicide is its reward. Kerry McSweeney gives a new dimension to the discussion of *The Great Victorian Collection* when he writes:

> The juxtaposition of past and present, old and new is the central structural principle in all four novels – [*An Answer from Limbo, I am Mary Dunne, Fergus and The Great Victorian Collection*] (as it was in Catholics) and the principal cause of the protagonists angst in three of them.[15]

But as an interplay of the poles of past and present, Dr. Maloney emerges the "centre of creative evolution" fighting a lost battle against the alienating elements that limit his choice in reality. Graham Greene as well as Brian Moore agrees with Henry Bergson on the prevalence of the past on the present moment while revolting against materialism.

> If the present moment contains no living and creative choice, and is totally and mechanically the product of the matter and motion of the moment before, then so was that moment, the mechanical effect of the moment that proceeded it and that again of the one before . . . and so on until, we arrive at the perennial nebula as the total cause of every later event of every line of Shakespeare plays and every suffering of the soul.[16]

Once we dispense with this epiphenomenon it is apparently a useless flame thrown up by the heat of the central commotion. We may consolingly hark upon Bergson's creative evolution. Duration is a continuous progress of the past which gnaws into the future and swells as it advances. It means that "the past in its entirety is prolonged into the present and abides there actual and acting."[17]

Doubtless we think with only a small part of our past: but it is with our entire past that we desire, will and act. And since time is an accumulation, the future can never be the same as the past for a new accumulation arises at every step. At least for a conscious being, to exist is to change, to mature is to go on creating ones self endlessly ". . . Perhaps all reality is time and duration, becoming and change. Consciousness seems proportionate to the beings power of choice in reality".[18] When a living being is the centre of action, it represents a sum of contingency entering into the world, that is to say a certain quantity of possible action. Man is no passively adaptive machine, he is a focus of redirected force a centre of creative evolution.

Thus Brian Moore's ingenuity in forging a Dr. Maloney elevated humanity to the realm of God's divinity and depicts man's mastery over matter, his image over the elements in a supreme moment of creative evolution.

But Michael Paul Gallagher remarks that the text poses deeper questions:

> Ever since the apparitions of Fergus Moore has allowed himself a certain obsession with the ghostly. The *Great Victorian Collection* is concerned with secular miracle but here he pushes in to further region of a religious miracle. His central question would seem to be whether a miracle can force a person into faith . . . miracles are only signs which solicit belief never a sign which compels assent to what preceded and what followed them and so to suggest to us that decision which is the most useful.[19]

But this is not all. By allowing us to grasp in a single intuition multiple moments of duration, it frees us from the movement of the flow of things, that is to say from the rhythm of necessity. The more these memories can contract into one, the firmer is the hold which it gives us on matter, so that the memory of a living being appears indeed to measure, above all, its powers of action upon thing. As Michael Paul Gallaher points out:

> If Dr. Maloney was a determinist this act would have been an automatic and mechanical resultant of pre-existing forces, motive would flow into action with lubricated ease. But choice on the contrary is burdensome . . . In man, man alone, consciousness breaks itself. But in the case of Dr. Maloney there is no deliberate human action and so it becomes a sort of secular miracle but not an act of creation.[20]

Other than the romantic element of *The Great Victorian Collection* Brian Moore here brings contrary phenomenons of essence versus existence, Mind versus matter. Where existentialists assert that "Existence precedes essence," Brian Moore brings in a unique case where essence takes the upper hand, without the deliberate collaboration of the agent. The collective unconscious, which is earned and learnt, becomes an impetus to bring out realistically the man within, the intentionality, the spirit, into the material realm. Form becomes matter in a purely vacant moment of the psyche, to the tragic dismay of the author himself. When we compare it with Querry's agony a similitude of existential surrounding or "encompassing" can be detected. Kerry McSweeney Comments: "It is on one level a grim fable about artistic integrity and its pitfalls, a shrewd allegory".[21] As Philip French says "it is about the situation of artist in contemporary society"[22]

Any original creation is a moment when essence begets existence and then the existential situation is a frying pan for the creator. *The Great Victorian Collection* dwells on this point.

To elicit the readers' response both Graham Greene and Brian Moore follow different paths while establishing the same thesis. The artist who finds his emptiness and complete personal loss is throwing away the glory and pleasure, in trying to get a new lease of life. But what he is trying to escape alienates him from life and eats his self-image and life itself. This is the story of Querry.

But in the case of Dr. Maloney he is like Querry primarily eaten up from within and is caught up in an anguish and getting exhausted in worry, dismay and uncertainty and finds himself a sleepless man just entering the door of death, even before it is opened, by poisoning himself.

Brian Moore too provides genuine and realistic human situations to surround the microcosm that is confronted by Dr. Maloney. Thus what could be a topic of arid reading is converted into an episode that carries "a soul view", by providing situations like self-criticism by the author, the advertisement by Veterman, consulting the Dutch Clairvoyant Dr. Johanes Fateme, the intimacy with Mary Anne, the interpolation of a family feud and his own mother's remark that his discovery is a foolish fake, Mary Ann's escape and

Veterman's quarrel and finally the death of Dr. Maloney himself, are a series of situations through which Brian Moore asks us to reflect on the essence – existential dichotomy. If essence asserts itself in any creation the encompassing situation reacts and how an artist can be a Christ crucified on the horizontal and vertical poles of tensions of life, left alone with a naked ego that has to break away from body, a cessation of existence, "the absurdity of life" as Querry says.

The aggravating element of his "egomania" which leads him to a pathological state is primarily his own family discord. There his half-life is set apart and he has no ground of security from his wife Barbara. From the professional side too there is no solace left; for, his mother warns him "If you don't go home you are going to lose the job" (GVC 96). Instead of a positive stroke or a cajole, the mother serves as a snake of suspicion that contributes to the self-condescension in him. She calls his collection a practical joke and comments about Mary Ann "So your secretary come with you to the bath room" and "you are smitten with a wall-eyed girl" (GVC 82).

While the research group testifies it as "the greatest style collection of victoriana to have been uncovered in this century" and "the first wholly secular miracle in the history of mankind," there is a call from Barbara which brings back the whole episode about what happened a year before and he is shocked by her voice into a surge of resentment.

The little respite that he had longed for, in the Beach for Frisbee exercise too fails. For Veterman collapses under the obsessive neurotic fear over Mary Ann's father. (8) "The University Campus organised a protest to reinstate Maloney at once" (GVC 100). This jostled in him a grip of crisis and fear. The conflict in his mind is depicted thoroughly when Brian Moore writes:

> Maloney stood up at the threshold of his room, his lamp lighting there every solid objects, objects which today existed only because he had dreamed them into life. How could anyone abandon such thing? It would be worse than neglect, it would be a crime (GVC 123).

Brian Moore, who celebrated the dictum "memento ergo sum" in I am Mary Dunne, is posing memory as a terrifying monster.

"This room is empty. No seventeen year whores parade here before waist coated gentry and Piccadilly swells. Three is no life in my creation. There are no living figures" (GVC 123). How can I give up my future happiness for a series of empty rooms?

He decided "he would dream of his future, a year from now." "As soon as he had decided this for a moment, like a thief, the collection slipped back into his mind" (GVC 124).

If he now dreamed of that future life, he might never see the collection again. Day dreaming of leaving it here in that part, he would be liking its destruction. "Fear gripped him. But I must not be giving, he thought. I must renounce the collection. I will renounce the collection. I will renounce the collection" (GVC 124). When he slept in this determination, though the erotic posture of Mary Ann appeared in the looking glass but he lay there "Trapped unable to a deflect his graze or turn off the monitor he lay for eight hours a prisoner of this banal and terrible spectacle. In the morning he woke, but he lay, fall down on the floor" (GVC 143).

In his taxi he shares his fear of something that may happen to the collection "His panic floated up full grown" (GVC 143). The intensity of this lose the reader experiences when he shares bed with his secretary but even here he is in the despicable grip of fear and panic. "But in that one giddy flush of desire panic returned like an attack of nausea, to float him down a new and vertiginous slope" (GVC 143).

Creation, if it is a compelling act that comes out of a determinism and necessity or if it is an impulsive act, the agent will be nowhere. For the conscious, sub-conscious and unconscious are not fully dominated by the will of the artist himself. Since he is deprived of any thoughtful reflection of reality, the external world poses an unformidable challenge. Sentiment, ideas, values and morality are tossed in the waves of normlessness. Thus ego mania is enhanced into a pathological stage, for the apex of creation – the image of god in man – when the perception of truth beauty and goodness are deprived of.

In this emptiness, there is nothing left to hark upon for a peace and serenity in the tumultuous moment of life. Thus absence of an internal illumination leads to ego mania and pathology is parabolically illustrated here. Self-dependence, as Emerson points out should be God dependence; but here, it is nausea, panic fear, excitement anxiety and sleeplessness that reigns the ego. In this metaphysical friction of being, the will has nothing for which it should stand and nothing in which it should stand. It has left with nothing to say that it is mine and therefore it ought to be. Kerry McSweeney writes:

> The Four novels set in the United States (*An Answer from Limbo, I am Mary Dunne, Fergus and The Great Victorian Collection* all have important features in common. They are rather more technically innovative than Ginger Coffey and the Irish novels, and the central characters are not ordinary people life Judith Hearne, Diarmuid, Gavin, Tomas and Ginger. . . . The juxtaposition of past and present, old world and new is the central structural principle in all four novels (as it was in Catholics) and the principal cause of the protagonists angst in three of them.[23]

On the third level of parabolic meaning the collection represents the pressure and the persistence of the past. Although Maloney is not made a Catholic and although his collection is made up of English artifacts, it is very hard to avoid going behind Maloney to his creator and interpreting the *The Great Victorian Collection* as another attempt on Moore's part to come to terms with his Irish Catholic past. A writer can only write about what he knows and Moore's creative field, like Fergus' apparitions, largely consists of his Irish Catholic past. But oates calls it differentially. He writes:

> Brian Moore's *The Great Victorian Collection* is a slender parabolic enterprise burdened with transparent and surely unsurprising, theme concerning ''appearance and reality''.[25]

Thus *The Great Victorian Collection* poses many questions the answers of which linger. An artist (creator) possesses the transcendence and the immanence of reality at the same time. In terms of existential philosophy the transcendent emergence of the creativity of man is either part of "Being-in-itself" or part of "Being-for-itself". The metaphysical and spiritual exigencies are rooted in him and any artistic creation emerging out of his internal reality is from the very cradle of his being and is materialized in the present. Thus past and present should culminate in him to give an integrity; and the integrated expression is the act of creation. Thus an act of creation should be the peak or the supreme point of personality integration. But in the case of Dr. Maloney instead of getting contentment and satisfaction in his achievement he finds himself an empty shell once the hatching is over. Thus, the fundamental question, is the ego an emptiness? Or is the artists self a complete loss in a creative act? And if so how can the artist's function be theologically rational and vindicated to mar the possible loss of an ego? How can the emptiness of agenius like Querry or Maloney be resolved? How can the conscious, sub-conscious and unconscious be harmonised to be an impetus to feed the furtherance of reality?

The Bible, particularly in the first chapter of Genesis alludes to the basic vocation of man when God commands Adam to name the elements of the world which He has created. It is to bring forth the essential glory of the raw matter, through humanization, by stamping the human dominion over matter by bringing out the usable, beneficent form through the creativity of man. It is nothing but the discovery of the image of God or the discovery of the power of God in man or the form in matter. Once this commission is executed, he becomes part of the plan that we should fight against the power of the mighty 'empire of fate', fight against the power of the mighty 'empire of fate', fight against any necessitating determining mechanical influence that stands against the freedom of man. When Jesus said "I have come to give you life, and to give it abundantly." He is the life-head that gives vigorous vitality to the creative life of man-always and always the procreant word of the world. Thus the theological call of man is not to be a monomaniac or ego maniac going on harbouring one single act of essence (as it happened to Maloney) but to be actively altruistic, to spiritualize the world.

The basic question for a creative artist as a prophylactic measure of life is how to possess more radiant health and be filled with a greater zest for useful living. Basically the answer lies in getting close to the stream of life—a common force that expresses itself in every creature through out all nature.

Without tapping this mighty force any creativity will end in doom. Thus, the theological absence or mere secular self of the artists like Querry in the *A Burnt-Out Case* and Maloney in *The Great Victorian Collection* and their ensuing agony in the face of the bad faith and other concomitant absurdities of life, seem to point to a gestalt. We must search for a positive reality that should serve a configurative point of ego for creative artists that can save them from atavistic self-absorbing and ego maniac tendencies to positive and creative altruism that proudly claim that authentic image of God in him.

The heroes of both Graham Greene and Brian Moore in *A Burnt-Our Case* and *The Great Victorian Collection* are deprived of the vital and essential ingredients of artists namely the aesthetic intuition, which Aurobindo Ghosh calls in *The Future Poetry*, "the Soul View".

The failure to withstand success and a failure to withstand a momentous creative energy into fruition and the agony of life in the disgusting facts, could be well confronted, if the agents were not completely left to the drive of their ego, but were inspired by the soul in the commitment to a faith or to a person in faith. The lack of psychic distance between Graham Greene and Querry has offended many of Greene's Catholic admirers. Evelyn Waugh's catholic sensibility was so outraged that he refused to write a review:

> The efficient doctor is an atheist. The faithful missionaries have given up all attempts to impose the moral law and are interested only in building and finance. A grotesque catholic layman seeks to impose mystical ideas on his adolescent wife. . . . It is the first time Graham has come out as specifically faithless. Pray God it is a mood, but it strikes deeper and colder.[24]

Greene in *Ways of Escape* defends his right as a catholic to treat "the loss of faith just as freely as the discovery of faith." He wrote to Waugh:

> With a write of your genius and insight I certainly would not attempt to hide behind the time-old gag—that an author can never be identified with his characters. Of course in some of Querry's reactions there are reactions of mine, just as in some of Fowler's reactions in *The Quiet American* there are reactions of mine. I suppose the points where an author is in agreement with his character lend what force on warmth there is to the expression. At the same time

> one can say that a parallel must not be drawn all down the line and not necessarily to the conclusion of the line. Fowler, I hope, was a more jealous man than I am I wanted to give expression to various states or moods of belief and unbelief.[25]

The fluidity of the grip of life in the artist and the changing moods of faith synchronised with each one's station in life are experiences of both Graham Greene and Brian Moore; so too is the absurd end.

Greene is akin to Brian Moore in the dream technique successfully employed by him in many of his novels: In the themes of the *A Burnt-Out Case* and *The Great Victorian Collection* and in the absurd end they agree of their specific modes. Querry remark is a case in point: "Self-expression is a hard and selfish thing. It eats everything, even the self." (BOC 48)

This is what is explicated in *The Great Victorian Collection*. Dr. Maloney too loses his interest in life and cannot dream any more; loses interest in sex and dies of sleepless nights.

The limitations and losses of these artists certainly point to the right interpretation of Love. "Love your neighbour as you love yourself" is the Christian dictum. Love involves of course, self-emptying, self-losing. Even Christ said "The one who loses his soul for my sake will find it." Losing is finding and giving is a getting. Such a satisfying interaction with the world is what is expected. Artistic expression is beauty. An intuitive vision of beauty must drive the artists to go on. But if a disproportionate identity of the world over the ego of man sets in, and if the ego is left alone in its drive, the possible result is elucidated by the both the novelists in the same manner. Kerry McSweeney comments on the *The Great Victorian Collection*:

> "It may also be taken to represent not only an artist's ruling passion but anyones fantasy which, if not

> controlled can grow to destructive proportions and to distort and suffocate reality."[26]

An artist must lose himself for the integrity of his knowledge and will. Beauty and wisdom which are inherently related, must be made to fuse into the formation of a new being which stands above the eventful days of man, where perspicacity functions as a centripetal form. This new being is the gain of this giving. The solitary search of the artist for that illumination of beauty and an intelligibility of a comprehensive nature compel him to shun the present and he may have to recourse to a "historical partners of the past" in a functional setting. Without this sacrifice no artist can express his writing self.

But caught up in the grip of tragic travails and paradoxes of life the heroes of *A Burnt-Out Case*, and *A Great Victorian Collection* fail to organize their minds from this sublime pinnacle of artistic and divinely illuminated minds. For, their ego overpowers and deludes the lucid vision of their mind, and the engrossing burden of life cannot be confronted with a spiritual outlook. Therefore, more than a nothingness of creativity, they betray an absence.

The anonymity and the nothingness of the artists as pointed out in all religions, form a kind of self-emptiness, and it is necessary to get a tinge of fire from the Supreme form for self-expression.

> The anonymity of the artist belongs to a type of culture dominated by the longing to be liberated from oneself. . . . Supreme achievement of individual consciousness is to lose or find (both words means the same) itself in what is both its first beginning and its last end: "Whoever would save his psyche, let him lose it" (Luke XVII: 33).
>
> Is it for the Christian to consider any work "his own", when even Christ has said that - I do nothing of

> myself" (John VIII: 28) . . . the traditional artist is not expressing himself, but a thesis that it is in this sense that both human and divine art are expressions, but only to be spoken of as "self expressions" if it has been clearly understood what "self" is meant . . . "the traditional artist is normally anonymous, the individual as such being only the instrument of the "self" that finds expression.[27]

The artistic protagonists discussed in this chapter are not only caught up in existential angst but also are deprives of the two aspects of the creative activity—the work of intellect and that of the "two in us" namely our spiritual or intellectual self and sensitive psycho-physical ego-work together. The integration of the work of art will depend upon the extent to which the ego is able and willing to serve the self, or if the patron and the workman are two different persons, upon the measure of their mutual understanding. St. Bonaventure points out that the work of art proceeds from the artist according to a model existing in the mind; which model the artist discovers (excogitat = cintayati) before he produces, and then he produces it as the predetermined. Moreover, the artist produces the external work in the closest possible likeness of the interior model."[28]

This want of the internal illumination or co-ordination of spiritual and psycho-physical ego of the artist is pointed out not only by occidental seers but also by great oriental mystics like Sri Aurobindo. When he writes about the poetic process, he clearly points out that poetic word is a vehicle of the spirit, the chosen medium of the soul's self-expression" Aurobindo writes:

> This highest intensity of style and movement which is the crest of the poetical impulse in its self-expression, the point at which the aesthetic, the vital, the intellectual elements of poetic speech pass into the spiritual, justifies itself perfectly, when it is the body

> of a deep, high or wide spiritual vision in to which the life-sense, the thought, emotion, the appeal of beauty in the thing is discovered and in its expression, rise on the wave of culminating poetic inspiration and pass into an ecstacy of sight.[29]

This should be the self-image of any Creator. But Querry and Maloney suffer from its absence and fall into the pit of existential nausea, and are trapped in despair, worry anguish and alienation. In them knowledge and will are poles apart and reason loses its insight in serving the mundane will.

This deliverance of knowledge from servitude to the will, this forgetting of the individual self and its material interest, calls for an intuitive grasp of the universals. The work of art is successful then, in proportion as it suggests the platonic idea or universal, of the group to which the represented object belongs. This artistic elevation of knowledge above the servitude of the will takes us to St. John's Gospel. In the beginning there was the Word; and it was with God; it was God. He was in the beginning with God and everything was created through him. Nothing was created without him (John 1:1-4) 30. Citing St. Augustine's resfactae . . . in artifice creates dicuntur vivere. St. Bonaventura recognizes:

> The analogy of the human and divine artificers, in both cases and pattern of what is to be made pre-exists in the maker's living mind, and is alive in it, and remains alive in it even when the 'factible' has become 'factum' or after it has been destroyed.[31]

In the traditional doctrine of two minds, the immediate and universal background against which these creative mode of ideas exist, is worked out. Accordingly:

> The first Mind in act, in itself, is its own act of being- is "apart from sensibles" "contemplative", "impassible", without remembrance and unmixed; it doesn't think, or rather, its thing is the thinking of

> thinking i.e. the principle and not the activity of thinking. It thinks only itself; thought and what is thought are one and the same Mind "becoming everything" is what it knows. It is eternal and beatific life, the life of God himself. The second mind is creative, and an efficient cause in that it makes everything; it is passible and mortal, and thinks of contingent things, not always of itself.[31]

In these distinctions of the theoretical from the practical mind and in the identification of the former (mind) with the life of God and of its thinking with its thesis or "word", we see St. John's words. The first principle is not so much "in the beginning," as "at the top" was the word, and the word was with God, and this word was God. The word, as Aristotle thinks is the first mind, that when in its act of being it thinks itself, Christ the word, the "Son of God," through whom all things were made and whom Augustine calls God's art, the art by which all things were made.

The oriental search of Indian Philosophy too asks the question:

> What was it the Brahma knew, whereby he became the all? It is replied, "in the beginning, verily, this [self] was Brahma, it knew just itself (*atmanam* – evavet), thereby it became the all". "And when is that Beatitude"? Nothing but mind (*mana eva*) verily, my kind, it is by his mind that he possesses himself of the woman (i.e., *Vac*, the voice theotokos), a son is born of her, in his image; that is his Beatitude verily, my king, the imperial, supreme Brahma is just mind. As expressed in Thomist phraseology, the generation of the son is vital operation, principio conjunctiva.[32]

The whole purpose of life has been that man should realize himself in this other or essential form "the ideal likeness" – which alone is the form of divinity.

This vital element of identification of the artist's mind with "The Mind" or with the "Created ones" is lacking in the protagonists presented in *A Burnt Out Case, The Great Victorian Collection* and *The Mangan Inheritance*. In the latter the hero is clearly in search of his self in a dead poete mandit, whereas Querry is searching in self, not in an identity to his achievements, but is in a flight; Anthony Maloney is also enmeshed in the contingencies of life, and verifies "Nicolas of Cusa's Docta Ignorantia while wholly relinquishing their own mind" corresponds to philos, "He that flees for refuge from his own mind, flees for refuge to the "mind of all things."[33] Their refuge in charity or art does not serve an enrichment in the protagonists mentioned in the thesis. A nausea sets in to open the gate of tragedy and death of the whole person. The empty ego that Mangan reaches, at the end of *The Mangan Inheritance* and the realisation of Mary Dunne that "I am the daughter of Dunne after all"; and the conflicting times of life, in *I am Mary Dunne* are similar to the internal reality of Pinkie in The Heart of the Matter, Raven in *A Gun for Sale*, and Andrews in *The Man Within*. In the protagonists whom we have seen their energy remains at the level of 'Eros' and their creativity ends in a mere self-loosening without a finding, whereas in case of Christian agape, identity is found in a shared Lord. This points to the existential need for a cosmic point where the self-emptying capacity of man demands a point of sublimation and satiation that fills the soul, and not those fetish ones that serve as a mere substitute gratification.

REFERENCES

1. D.J. Enright and *Ernst De Chikera*, English *Critical Texts* (Harmondsworth: Oxford UP, 1962) 296.
2. *Ibid.*, 301.
3. Ananda K. Coomaraswamy, *Christian and Oriental Philosophy of Art* (Delhi: Munshiram Manohar Lal, 1974) 43.
4. *Ibid.*, 180.

5. *Ibid.*, 24.
6. *Ibid.*, 24.
7. *Ibid.*, 24.
8. V.S. Sethuraman, *Contemporary Criticism: An Anthology* (Madras: Macmillan, 1989) 267.
9. Frank Kermode, *Mr. Greene's Eggs and Crosses puzzles and Epiphanies* (London: Routledge, 1962) 180.
10. Seturaman, *op. cit.* 248.
11. *Ibid..*, 255.
12. Arthur Koestler, *The Act of Creation* (New York: Dell, 1987) 196.
13. Carl Gustav Jung, *Collected Works* (London: Fontana 1983) 239-40.
14. *Ibid..*, 13.
15. Kerry McSweeney, "Brian Moore Past and Present", *Critical Quarterly*, 18.2 (1976) 53.
16. Will Durant, *The Story of Philosophy* (New York: Washington Square, 1953) 450.
17. *Ibid..*, 45.
18. *Ibid..*, 45.
19. Michael Paul Gallagher, "Rev. of Cold Heaven", *Irish University Review* 14.1 (1986) 131-32.
20. *Ibid..*
21. Kerry McSweeney, *Brian Moore: Past and Present* 53.
22. Philip French, "The Novels of Brian Moore", *London Magazine* (Feb. 1986) 86-91.
23. Kerry McSweeney, *op. cit.*, 58-59.
24. Joyce Carol Oates. *Take of Love and Idolatry* (New York Book Rev. 2 Aug. 1981) 3.
25. Michael Paul, *The Diaries of Evelyn Waugh* (London: Nicholson, 1976) 779.
26. Kerry McSweeney, *op. cit.*, 53.
27. Ananda K. Coomaraswamy, *What is Civilization* (New Delhi: Oxford University Press, 1989) 180.
28. *Ibid..*, 184.

29. Aurobindo Ghosh, *The Future Poetry* (Pondichery: Sri Aurobindo Ashram, 1991) 255.
30. *The Holy Bible* John 1:1-4.
31. Coomaraswamy, *op.cit.*, 180.
32. *Ibid..*, 179.
33. Coomaraswamy 184.

4 THE WILLING SPIRIT AND THE WEAK FLESH

A thematic division of Greene's or Brian Moore's works is bound to be arbitrary. But there is an unvarying tenor in the midst of shifting emphasis in each novel which as Greene said, is "the ruling passion" that gives "to a shelf of novels the unity of a system."[1] Their intense concern is with the loss of the dignity of human action. This loss has resulted from the concomitant loss of religious sense. Graham Greene laments this, when he writes on Francois Mauriac: "For with the death of James the religious sense was lost to the English novel and with the religious sense went the sense of the importance of the human act."[2] Brian Moore too feels the same when he writes:

> I found when I started to write, I became very interested in the question of faith . . . the virtue of having a belief in something. I began to see and feel, as I do now, that the great lack of modern life is a lack of a belief in something greater than ourselves.[3]

The domestic, social and intellectual milieu that the protagonists of the Belfast novels of Brian Moore try to evade are parallel to the social and ethical dimensions that the protagonists of Graham Greene's novels are engrossed in. The question of faith that Brian Moore tries to tackle in these novels too is similar to the religious sense that Graham Greene probes in his fictions. Both look upon the dichotomy of the will—the rational elicit appetite – and the flesh in their mundane "encompassings" as one opposes the other. The will is attuned to a "willing suspension of disbelief" taking any opportunity, either miraculous or secular. But the flesh, both in its carnal tendencies and concupiscences, ties down the dynamism of the spirit through the will. The spiritual soaring of the will and the incapacity of men to follow up that surge and getting entangled in flesh is the grim phenomena of life that can be seen in the fictions of both Graham Greene and Brian Moore. Whereas the whole of the early heroes and heroines of their fictions grapple with the inhibitive dimensions of flesh, in the later ones, there is a deliberate dominance of the spirit over flesh. Thus the early as well as the later novels of Graham Greene and Brian Moore pose the question 'To believe or not to believe'.

In *The Man Within* (1924) *It's a Battlefield* (1934) and *England Made Me* (1935), the terror stricken characters seem to grope in darkness for an anchorage to hold on. The escaping father figures, the insufficient and ever-wanting romantic moments, the insatiable point of justice and the baffled faces of loyalties are simply "the nearer the beginning" of a quest. But the frightening milieu of this search has a golden optimistic end on the solid rock of God, though religion and faith seem, in this phase, very faint and can even be relegated. Derek Traversi, for example, does not see any link in the emotions of the protagonists with religion and faith:

> That emotions of this kind have any necessary connection with religious belief is open to question. Beyond the intense feeling generated by personal resentment, religion is only present as a kind of mechanical superstition, involving the appeasement of forces imperfectly discerned but associated with the relentless persecution of the individual by the herd . . . and, once "life" has been in some obscure way equated with the operations of destiny, the only possible defence is a gesture of propitiation, the adherence to

> a rite which is itself imposed upon the individual as something incomprehensible and alien.[4]

Having no hope, the protagonists of the earlier novels are invariably haunted by a sense of fear and failure baptized in the intimations of evil quite early in life. For Andrew, school was a prison, through the glass door of the headmasters' room. Conrad Drover got the original hurt to his sensibility across the desk:

> "Conrad sat at the desk aware of the hatred behind him in the school, in the office: the cold recognition of his efficiency through the glass door of the head master's room, of the managers room; Conrad earned six polands a week" (IB 59).

The marred egos of men searching for a form, take in turn the apprehension of evil, linking the ephemeral and the eternal, the empirical and the metemperical, the tangible and the intangible, the physical and the metaphysical. The ethical and the theological co-exist and complement one another by a curious contrast in Greene's later novels called the "Catholic trilogy."

By juxtaposing, Pinkie—'the incarnation of pure evil' and Rose and Ida's ideas of "right and wrong", as David Lodge writes, Greene achieves "an extraordinary displacement of conventional values and sympathies."[5] In Brighton Rock Whether it is the murder of Hale or Spicer or the "Carving Up" of Brewer, he is the embodiment of ruthlessness. "Life for him was a series of complicated tactical exercises, as complicated as the alignments at Waterloo thoughtout on a brass bedstead among the crumbs of sausage rolls. . . . How could you think out a larger strategy under those conditions?" (BR, 112). The deviant delinquent mind is beautifully exposed out in oxymoronic terms: "He felt desire more again like nausea in the belly and his virginity straightened in him like sex" (BR 85-90). The intimacy "sickened him like the idea of age" (BR 101); yet he locks

Rose in a "brutal, now-or-never embrace" (BR 181). From wed-lock to bed-lock Pinkie's is a flight from "an embryo of sensuality to the last human shame" (BR 181). So even in the intimacy of love he is a man of guilt and cruelty. Thus away from the sympathy as well as empathy of people, the escathological dimension challenges the human promulgations in laws.

Raven in *A Gun for Sale* has always been conscious of his own ugliness. For Raven, his hare lip is like a badge of class. It reveals the poverty of parents who could not afford a surgeon. He inspires repulsion in others. Together with his physical deformity, his consciousness is conditioned by a father hanged in Wandsworth prison and a mother with her throat cut. So murder does not mean much to Raven. It is just a new job. He is now hired as an assassin by a firm of armament manufacturers, to kill the head of a European State. The two hundred pounds which he receives at the end of his business, is reported as stolen money and Raven is on the run. He comes across an actress with whom the police inspector in charge of the case is in love. Raven's plan to make use of her and kill her is defeated by her absolute trust and compassion. He tells her all and convinces her of his sincerity. She believes him and wants to prove her trust; but in the end she betrays him—the last of a series of betrayals. Raven's defeat in Annie is equal to that of Andrews who "longed for peace and beauty and the minutes were flying by and he was still a fugitive, with mind muddled and obscured by fear of death (MW 32).

The question of faith that Brian Moore tries to tackle in his novels too is similar to the religious sense that Graham Greene deals with in his fictions. Brian Moore too takes a negative and positive approach to life throughout the earlier and later novels to enable the readers to see life lived out in flesh and to recognize the urge of the spirit. As O' Donoghue writes:

> Both *Judith Hearne* and *The Feast of Lupercal* are anti-religious and anti-Catholic, because religion, far from liberating or empowering Judith Hearne or Diarmuid Devine, is the power that enslaves them. It is not merely a spiritual slavery, though that too exists, but because the society they live in (the Catholic portion of Belfast Society) has adopted completely the tenets of Catholicism, particularly the repression of sexuality, and has hardened and codified these tenets into social interdiction. It is the slavery of the whole personality or even of the unconscious psyche.[6]

About *Judith Hearne* Brian Moore writes:

> I felt that in *Judith Hearne* I had written about somebody losing faith and it then occurred to me to ask, what was the education, the religious education and the background, which may be destroyed that woman's life-she was a 'Sacred Heart' girl. And so I become interested in a school character and in how much that kind of education makes cowards of us all-because we have to live in the community, we can't just walk away from it.[7]

The powerlessness of the individual in a Catholic society produces certain stereotyped persons. Una's comments on her married lover reveals this:

> That's what's worried me all along. I'm the one who's taken all the risks in this thing. He's just like a lot of Irishmen I know. He pretends to be a wild Celt but he's frightened to do anything his neighbour's wouldn't approve of (FL 75).

Brian Moore's *Judith Hearne* like Andrew and Raven, is a victimised ego, born and brought up in a narrow rigid set up of bigotry. The author himself testifies:

> I discovered in writing it what I really felt about my past. I left Ireland with the intention of not going

> back, but my reasons became clear only when I wrote my first novel. It was then my bitterness against the begetting in Northern Ireland, my feelings about the narrowness of life there, and in a sense my loneliness when living as an exile in Canada all focussed to produce a novel about what I felt the character of ulster to be.[8]

Judith Hearne illustrates the social phenomena in individual existence. *Judith Hearne*, the spinster, in her solitude is in a rooming house in post-war Belfast, with a picture of the sacred Heart and her dead aunt D'Arcy and a perpetual bottle of cheap whisky to assist her through the bad times. She is another Raven battered by the bruising narrowness of the interactions and bigotry of her religion. While her solitude elicits compassion, her sense of martyrdom and melodrama and nullifying humility make her pathetic. She shares the indomitable will and audacity to rebel against with Greene's heroes. The fiery proud that shapes the content of her character is the marrow of her life. She rebels against god and society and at last she too reconciles with the fallen world. The alienated individual, in her social repression counts even religion as waterless oasis to quench the dried ego. Existential anguish (angst) is perpetrated and perpetuated by repression socially and religiously; for even religion fails to provide faith. Thus the basic Canadian question 'where are we here?' reverberates in our ears. Judith's attitude towards religion itself is based on observance rather than belief. When Judith and Madden go to Mass Judith's religious attitude is made very clear:

> She was not, she sometimes childed herself, a particularly religious person. No, she had followed her aunt's lead in that. Church affairs, her aunt once said, tend to put one in contact with all sorts of people whom one would prefer not to know socially. Prayer and rigorous attention to ones religious duties will contribute far more towards ones' personal salvation

than the bickering that goes on about church bazaars . . . Religion was there (JH 12).

Jo O'Donoghue comments:

the attitude revealed in this passage is a most joyous mixture of snobbery, devotionalism and observance without any solid basis on any real sense of transcendence or spirituality.[9]

Father Quigley in all his cursory and mumbled prayers in English and Latin is a professional cleric who makes mass a routine. He is a combination of all defects imaginable in a Catholic priest and the sermon is a laughable dramatic event

They have got time for sin, time for naked dancing girls in the cinema, time to get drunk . . . time to spend hours making up their football pools . . . Except one. They don't have time for God (JH 64)[10]

In the confessional box, the priest was a pathetic figure interested in political power:

But she stopped speaking. She had seen his face. A weary face, his cheek resting in the palm of his hand, his eyes shut. He is not listening, her mind cried. Not listening (JH 172).

For James Madden her lover, the anchorage of faith is lost: "Religion was insurance, it meant you got your security awards" (JH 58) These are the same religious sentiments of Graham Greene's heros—Raven, Andrews and Pinkie too.

In exploring the victimisation of the individuals, Graham Greene and Briar Moore are hand in hand. Andrew's social mooring is cut off in his father figure; so is the case of Raven who is simply a hired murderer who realizes that not even a modicum of dignity is left in the world of robbers. Pinkie too is chased after by his own internal awareness of corruption and external malignant acts. His friends and even wife are mere stepping stones of an unrealised ego. His world is limited to theft, espionage and betrayal even in marriage. Judith Hearne's world is a sordid one replete with narrowness. Her drinking friend Edie is in Earnscliff Home—an institution for indigent women. Sunday friends – the O' Neills, indulges her with hospitality. Her lover James Madden wants only a business partner to Americanize Ireland. Fat Bernard and his doting mother, her land lady, oppresses her. The Church offers an empty ritual and indifferent God. All she has, to help her to cope with doubt and despair, is her pride and her bottle.

Her fall is a spectacular event. She gets drunk in the best hotel in Belfast defying her own sense of frugality, propriety and decorum and then she assaults the tabernacle on the Church altar. She feels certain that her prayers were always unheard. Having burnt all bridges behind her, Judith finds ambivalent salvation in the anesthesia of acceptance.

In one of the strongest Catholic countries in the world, here is a figure deprived of any solace either in culture or religion or in social interaction and falls victim to the fallen world. Harassed and harangued by objectivisation, the hero finds that

> Religion was insurance. It warrants you got security awards. It meant you could always turn over a new leaf. . . . He found it comforting to start out as often as possible with a clean slate, a new promising figure (JH 58).

Quoting Terry Eagleton, O' Donoghue asserts on the Society of Judith that a drably detailed grimly unselective reproduction of life as it is of the seedy realm of routine social existence. This is the same seediness with Graham Greene tries to project in the social milieu of his early novels.

Hallvard Dahlie aptly calls Judith Hearne a "dirge for a spinster and a city." In the ultimate scene of blasphemy where

Judith tries to open the tabernacle door "open let me in!" and in the response she gets:

> He came out, terrible, breathing fire, his face hollow-cheeked, his eyes devouring her. . . . And He, His fingers uplifted in blessing bent over her, his bleeding heart red against his white tunic. Lifted her in his arms and his face was close to her (JH 211).

Jeanne Flood viewing the Soul's basic urge for the transcendental reality here, writes:

> The question of the vacancy of the tabernacle or to overwhelming fullness lies at the centre of Moore's work, for that question are tied two others with which he has struggled in his novels, out of which he has created his novels. With the fullness of tabernacle, moore associates an objective world which is created and ordered by a father whose absolute power is synonymous with a terrible Sadistic energy. With its emptiness he associated a void in which a silly, person floats, trapped forever in his solipsistic dread. On the great presence or great absence depend the reality of the world outside the mind and the legitimacy of the novelists, commitment to his own imagination.[11]

This vacancy or the great absence in the mind of Judith is 'The within' from which she flies. The within and the without are equal to both Judith and Andrews. Just as Raven's ego is encompassed and throttled by the injustice of robbers, Devine's individuality is stifled by an unjust and imposing educational system that forces itself at the detriment of persons. Thus from the "Claustrophobia of Judith's life" Brian Moore moves on in his, *The Feast of Lupercal* "to a concern with the catholic influence on education and border society. Devine does not get maturity enough to be independent and above the system, but he does not rebel against or defy the system openly as it is done by Judith. For there is a systematic recurrent effort designed and maintained by the clerical masters of Adrath to prevent any individual master or boy from valuing his own independence and maturity. Devine and their masters enforce this system when they have power in the class room. Devine's love affair with Una Clarke—like that of Raven's affair with Anne—is to escape from the throttling influence of a society.

As a person he is both old and new. What makes him caught up in the old world is, the Victorian waist coat, his father's signet ring, and the Victorian moustache, all mark him as being attached to the past. Through the length of his hair and loudness of his socks, he appears young, but he is called old woman. His self-confidence is shaky and Connolly remarks:

> That he was some ninny, incapable of getting a girl. As for girls, well, he had never been a ladies man. He was not ugly no, not too shy, no, but he never had much luck with girls. It was the education in Ireland, damn't it, he had as it many a time. He had been a boarder at this very same school, shut off from girls when they left school (TFL 15).

Together with the imposing impotency of the systems, imposing father figures too cow him down by years of conditioning. Father McSwiney is an authoritarian father figure. "Father McSwiney seemed an impossible opponent remembered from childhood, twice as large as life. There was no hope of changing the authoritarian mind (FL 45).

In a brave moment he falls in love with someone outside his system – Una Clarke. "It's astonishing the confidence she gave me: I was a different man (FL 55). But the man in Ardath knew that this relationship with Una as "materialistic values of self-love, neglecting your duty as a catholic" (FL 82). But he too does not have the maturity to succeed, for when he is going to bed with Una, he is sick as a boy who is not prepared; the role has been reversed, he is victim. The principal's use of the big stick is the degradation of Devine despite his clamour: "I am a grown man I will not be treated like a school boy (FL 228) but he is treated as a boy in their leniency, ignoring of the rumours.

Even in the little freedom of choice of Una, in a conditioned educational background, his individuality stands little chance. Jo O'Donoghue writes:

> In this he is like Judith Hearne . . . like Judith Hearne's, it is the voice of the determined character who has been made weak and unfree by the combination of personality, habit, education and by the highly repressive social educational system presided over by the catholic clergy and which it would take much stronger man than Devine to resist.[12]

Thus it is the story of the powerlessness of the individual in a society—the Catholic society. The repressed ego that lost its self-image – (God image) – points to the lack to what is to be compensated for. Catholic ethics and etiquette succeed only to mould a repressive ego that limits one to the narrow view of life that does not know the omniscient view of universal tolerance and unity, to keep unity and balance in any mode of society.

The critical honesty of the author to deprive the ego of the repressing and blurring phase of the superstructure of the Catholic Church begs a transcendental and spiritual vision to purge the ego of its impediments to enjoy a freedom and divinity rooted in faith. Thus both Graham Greene and Brian Moore basically drive at a faith that sublimates and supplements a natural ego, as well as at an education that is loyal to the etymology that adducer suggests. Education should be a leading out, either in its noetic, moral or aesthetic aspect. It is an appeal to a faith that stands above a system, a structure, a scheme of affairs. It aims at a faith that can absorb all moments of life. Thus, both Judith and Devine Darmund from their inferiority or from their introvert life of the soul surge and soar above the powerful and compelling influence of a system.

This is exactly the case of Ginger Coffey, in *The Luck of Ginger Coffey*: the Dubliner who in his middle age, with great aspirations and no money at all settles in Montreal with his wife Veronica and their daughter Pauline.

Ginger has no choice but to follow the indeterminate chain of events as they arise. Thus in the sea of life, rejected as a neophyte executive, he tries journalism and ends up as a proof-reader and also makes deliveries for a diaper service on the side. Even his married life teeters towards failure. His wife is in love with a cartoonist, a caricature of what a man should be. Yet Ginger fails to fulfil the requirements of life. Critic O'Donoghue sees him as "unrealistically optimistic". He squanders the emergency money of his family. He becomes a "self-deluder" "hopelessly incompetent", a person who has freedom to do what he wants with his life; but does not know what he wants to do. Like a boy he hides, to escape the consequence of his responsibility.

The Church does not calcify him. He is not advised to take moral deliberations and decisions. He is positively against the stubborn and bullying tactics of the church. He challenges the birth control policy of the church. When he approaches the church for warmth, he exhibits his defiance aggressively. He deliberately evades the attempt of the church to reclaim him.

The more his incapacity to face the needs of life emerges, the more he plunges into the abyss of despair. Just as in all the novels of Brian Moore, Ginger too faces the moment of crisis when he is put on trial for urinating in a public place, for which he receives a six months' suspended sentence. This is the time when his integrity of personality is greatly recognized in him by his wife. Ginger renews the marriage and tries to be a man of the world.

In the case of Ginger, what we ask is, 'where is that self-image which can be constructive in its keeping of integrity. Why does man feel an indispensable passivity? Is there not a point of zest that makes him go forward in spite of the discrepancies of life? Why do the marital and social elements incapacitate the man? What has happened to the will power of man? Is it that man is passively bound to their situation by only partially controllable forces?

The final tantalizing question posed by Ginger is why, despite all the alienating influences—family, Church and society, as revealed in the petty mean drab lives of sharply defined secondary characters like the grizzled proof-reader, Old Billy, or iron pumping Warren K. Wilson—does Ginger equip, himself for a renovative moral choice and calcified life? The only answer is his vision in an ego that has a mooring beyond the family, society and social strictures, conventions and taboos. The luck and plenty that he has enjoyed even in a dissociating immigrant experience, is a vision, a gestalt that Moore gives us in all the heroes who are caught up in a crisis. It is a pattern that is based on extra-mundane, metempirical reality. When his personal integrity is accepted he adjusts to life. As Seaums Deane remarks, "It is here Moore begins to free himself from the simplise of the battle between the aspiring individual and stifling social form."[13] Although Judith Hearne and Devine discover their lost childhood, Ginger Coffey does not find a saving paternity in the church and its patrimony.

Graham Greene takes departure from lost childhood, crime and guilt to global problems and prophetic roles in the characters of his later novels. In *Stamboul Train* where Dr. Czinner, a tired middle-aged man who single-handedly wages war against a tyrannical regime, the sense of justice gets an exponent. In his speech before Colonel Hartep who is the representative of the reactionary forces of law Czinner argues: "You are employed to bolster up an old world which is full of injustice and muddle . . . you put the small thief in prison but the big lives in palace"[14] Again he says "the wealth of the world belong to every one. If it was divided, there would be no richness but every one would have no reason to feel ashamed beside his neighbour." (ST 201)

Conder, the crime journalist in *Its a Battlefield* is a matured version of Dr. Czinner. He had spent his life in learning the incomprehensibility of those who judged and pardoned, rewarded and punished:

> The world was run by the whims of politician, a journalist, a bishop and a policeman. They hanged this and pardoned that; one embezzler was in prison but the other men of the same type were sent to parliament (IBF 39).

So these heroes of the earlier novels and entertainments question the parental figure, the ethical plane, and social structure. Commenting on Greene's entertainer, David Pryce-Jones remarks that *A Gun for Sale*, *The Confidential Agent* and *The Ministry of Fear* are not merely entertainments. "All of them have something of a moral theologian's disputations about them".[15]

These features which are the dominant tenets of the earlier novels of Greene are lengthened and deepened in the ensuing novels too. Conventional morality is displaced and inverted when Arthur Rowe in *The Ministry of Fear* instigated by pity kills first his wife and then his enemy. This pity gets its vehemence in *The Heart of the Matter*. The figure 'D' in *The Confidential Agent* despite the distrust of his party, undertakes a suicidal and hopeless mission. Like Maurice Castle in *Human Factor*, he is torn between loyalties: loyalties to an abstract system, ideology and to individual human beings. Thus these "torn-withins," emaciated and depersonalized by social pressure, despite all the tragic tones, tunes and fleeting rhythms of life, are really heading for a point, an order, both within and without.

The wealthy, bored young Oliver Chant, the hero of *The Name of Action* finds a meaning in life by financing a revolution. But when he is infatuated with the wife of the dictator, Anne Marie Demassener, personal values and political motives get confused. But when Chant questions his lieutenant, Weber, the latter refers to the infallible standard of the Catholic Church as the source of their loyalty. Catholicism for Weber is above the mundane, offering the place of certainty and security.

Weber's wife is the embodiment of Catholic solidity. She can speak with a certainty never troubled by needs, questionings, doubts, analysis. That, is a haven to which neither Chant nor Anne-Marie Demassener can ever come. They were born in an age of doubt and to a class which wished to know too much. Chant's heritage is a modern one, a dry rationalisation which offers him little comfort. He and his generation have lost contact apparently irrevocably, with the spiritual certainly possessed by Frauweber. In an attempt to still and satisfy the needs, he places his hopes first in political action, then in sexual love. Both fail him and the recognition of failure comes to him in a Church where God was not a cloudy aspiration but a concrete hope or fear. He has believed in freedom, he has believed in love, it has seemed to Chant that he has been enabled to see the boundaries of the infinite. The twentieth century skepticism, which has moulded Chant's personality presents commitments to the mysterious faith which will resolve his spiritual crisis and offers him the certainty he requires. It is the emotions that draw him towards commitment and the intellect and the curses of doubt and analysis, hold him back. He belongs to a generation of explainers but the power of Catholicism is presented as quite unexplainable. Here Catholic belief assumes a power for certainty and identity. Brian Moore's protagonists too liberate them from the insular forces of paternity, sex and schools to global and ethical problems.

Another Moore hero who is baptized in the cold and rebellious waters of Belfast is Gavin Burke in *The Emperor of Ice-Cream*. The existential cataclysm from which the protagonist tries to escape is parallel to the situations of Judith, Devine and Ginger Coffey. The only difference is that he is convinced of his calling as a social reformer, with a vision of a changed morrow like the historical vision of W.B. Yeasts. He is equal to Czinner, and Conder in his reformist zeal.

He too stands against three forces for ultimate freedom and maturity - sexual, religious and intellectual. Sally Shannon, his wife, is another strain in the domicile front. What can a family life with her, despite an intense attraction to her bring forth? Something similar to his father's personality torn between his love for law and love for Sally. Thus he is harangued by the twin traumas of love and hate. He is between the devil of rebellion due to the love of knowledge and the deep sea of pure love.

The Victorian, Catholic and Nationalist father is another figure he is in conflict with. His failure in matriculation is used by the father as an opportunity to exercise control and not to canalize the energy into a new role. His father's trade relation with uncle Tom has no sincerity in it. Thus, a cold pedantic legalistic patrimony that oscillates between solicitor tradesman or the ARP fills Gavin with indecision. He finally decides not to go with the family to Dublin. The relationship is resolved in the blitzes of family.

The vision of a new world order that he cherished with Yeats, Louis Macanzie, Clifford Oddels, and Wallace Stevens, is nothing but the projected but unrealised ego of his father. Thus the alienation assumes a prophetic role.

What was assumed as an apocalyptic vision of escape take a surreal phase in Fergus. Here too the escape of the rigid psyche is for a universal.

Fergus Fadden is a vacant soul in a Waste land near Los-Angelos far away from the motherland—Ireland. Self-excommunicated from Catholicism by religious belief and life style, he is now in search of a self. No one can escape, it seems to be suggested, when he is beleaguered by the crowded memories of the past family. The exile calcifies him to adolescence. His lust with dentists—wife and rebellion against education and religion takes him to a trauma. The last apparition of the day is his father—Catholic traditional and authoritarian. His consorting with movie moughuls and girls half his age and the girls parent's agony contribute to the burden of his ego. The agony of existence of the past and the presence pose the question of identity and beg for a life style.

The historical tension of the past and present in the eternal flow of time and the existential nausea to which he is drive to through an insufficient and rigid patrimony produces in the hero, a thirst for an identity at the expense of the past. His search is for a value system of his own different from that of the moorings of his own family. Andrew of *The Man Within*, and Pinkie of *The Brighton Rock* and Raven of *A Gun for Sale* are all on the same track of search like the heroes of the Belfast novels.

Another hero, Anthony Maloney, of the *The Great Victorian Collection*, the doctor historian, is a professor of university. But archeological investigation has led him to the hotel in Carmel. The already estranged family life and sense of loneliness is deepened by the newspaper report that he has dreamt out a miraculous reality. Absolute escape gives him a dream, an ephemeral reality. No man, let alone Antony Maloney can stand a life unless he is audacious enough to solve the problem of his soul through a creative approach to life. He too is caught up in domicile, social and existential conflict and "the overdose of barbiturates combined with alcohol is the potent symbol of modern mans' angst and the spiritual vacuum in which he lives."[16] In *The Mangan*

Inheritance James Mangan embarks on a quest. For he is in an identity crisis.

So he is on his way of confirming his destiny as a poet, through his link with the nineth-century poete' mandit, James Clarence Mangan. As soon as he arrives the west Cork, in search of inheritance, quite helplessly he watches his own life slithers out of his control while in Drishne. In this bid for self-importance, he ultimately realizes that inheritance and qualities are outside ones own control as ones' appearance. No escape from self and no new identity in the past. The painful self awareness is bloomed in him that he would never have to doubt his qualities and the past.

Loss of identity: not to be compensated in past, nor in inheritance nor in personal qualities, then where?, except in the Other – is the pattern equal to the salvation of Greene's heroes. If the mid is rooted in the other – the unfaiting treasure it will always be a glittering Light House.

In *The Doctors Wife* the ego and self-image of Sheila Redden are undergoing the excruciating pain of the exile experience. She is a lapsed Catholic living in Ireland, an exile manque, who would have left Ireland long before. But for her husband she would have never stayed in Ireland. She says to her brother, "I always was at home here. (Paris)" I don't feel at home, at home" (DW 18). Her attraction to her uncle is "to sail away from all of the things that held and bind me, to sail away, to start again in some city like Brussels or Amsterdam (DW 40). This sailing of soul is augmented by the violent phase, the troubles of Ireland took. Exile experience thus becomes a necessity for the happiness of life. This longing for the exile experience is the Soul's search for a universal that shines above the rigidity of parochialism provincialism and the subcultural values and norms. She does not want to be 'a functional woman'- in terms of existentialist philosophy. She does not find her identity in being in the shoe of her husband – the doctor. The question left to us is, which is the final anchorage of this sailing soul?

In *An Answer from Limbo* (1968) Brendan Tierney's quest is for glory beyond the posh aspects of life, religion and domesticity. The central consciousness of this novel is the guiltless and the unsympathetic personality of Brendan moving to the obsessive pinnacle of self-dependence. The core of his ambitious personality is revealed as: "my course was set towards a destiny I have not yet accomplished. In that dream I weep."(AFL 10)

Thus, rooted in the past and planning for the future, Brendan Tierney appears an image of the omnipotent God. Like wine through water, through Brendan Tierney as a man, a son, and a husband runs his obsession, to be a writer. This calcifies him to an indifferent being:

> When I leave my work room, I enter into a state of waiting. At home I walk room to room, I pick up books but do not read them. . . . The apartment is blessedly peaceful; no rows, no children, no television. The children are in Saratoga and my mother of course, is at Finnerty's apartment. As for Jane . . . She will be going back up to Saratoga again to see them this weekend and I've the apartment completely to myself. Peace it's wonderful." (AFL 249)

Brendran is a completely dehumanized being. His wife being estranged by silence, his mother dejected, children away, showing no elation at any moment of life, he is deeply involved in negotiations and discussions with Gerston or Solsilver. When he wears his destiny as a writer he articulates a sense of loss for humanity. Thus he objectives his experience, and he in turn is objectivised. We are invited to look at him. His detachment paves way for his greatness. Bereft of mundane elements of life he wants to communicate to the other. But what is that other?

Mrs. Tierney, in her parochial and narrow Catholicism, is often hurt by taunting words and thus prepares for the estrangement and the neglect which results in her death. She is a victim of powerlessness, unconcerned, uncared for, she dies isolated, paralysed by a stroke.

Thus, the three central voices have no quality of truth and no genuine self-forgetfulness. Here is a protagonist who is cramped from within as well as from without, resulting in a complete vacuum of ego. No glory is left with to relate to others on a human footing. All the novels discussed so far present protagonists whose interior egos are so much a cauldron of activity that they try to escape in to a liberating point other than society, politics, religion and domestic life.

In *I am Mary Dunne* Mary's day unfolds in an aura of suppressed hysteria, in the form of the conscious reconstruction of the day just passed while she lies in bed beside her third husband, Terrence Lavery, a successful British playwright with whom she lives in New York. That morning, disoriented in parts by premenstrual anxiety, she forgets her name at the hairdressers. In Mary's ruminating mind the action ranges from analytic to confessional; she recounts the harrowing quest for her identity. She has been Mary and Maria, Mary Dunne, Mary Phelan, Mary Bell, Mary Lavery. She takes us to the "Jaurez Dooms"—her term for the feelings of depression she experiences following her divorce from Hat Bell. She exults in her love for Terence and riles at her luncheon with Janice Solan, who helped undermine her marriage to Hat, cringes at the obnoxious mauling of her ex-suitor Ernie Truelove. This is the exploration of herself without trying to make connection. In the end it is accepted behind all these guises that there is a whole woman, that all the roles are contained by the personality who plays them.

All her isolation, spiritual poverty and psychological dissociation lead her to the final realization that honesty to oneself becomes the only saving grace.

In the circular voice of Mary, a guilty conscience is brought out. Her longing for a humanistic form of secular happiness ends in guilt which has no beginning and no end. The actual narrative of her day, this Thursday in New York, is logical; it proceeds through the morning hair appointment, through lunch, to the next evening. It is a frenzied inner discourse which represents her as actress, as pander, as whore. Her inner personality is always in conflict with the outer: "Maybe I am not promiscuous, but I have been married three times and I am only thirty two. Maybe without my knowing it, I am old Dan Duyes' daughter after all" (VD 78).

Her sense of guilt leads her to embrace irrationality and isolation. Duality is dissolved here. The individuals perception of his own guilt and his own responsibility are formed by all elements that influence the human psyche including heredity, memory and religion. Her identity is sought in the dead father, and in this he assumes the father figure who stands above to absorb the guilt of his daughter and grant her identity.

An internal personality that does not share anything with the world experienced so far as its point of reference, is a self-illuminated ego that shares its light from above. The fundamental questions Brian Moore asks in the Belfast novels are embodied and enlarged with deeper insights and ontological perception in the protagonists of the later novels.

These protagonists are not mere objective correlatives of personal freedom or persons seeking liberation. It is not simply a freedom of choice, but a freedom that comes on a par with the Sartrean concept which insists that man has to "determine not just actions but his identity". In Doctor's Wife Sheila Reddens identity is derives from someone else – (rather a profession than a person). She has to choose not simply her actions but her own being. There is a difficulty in establishing a rapport between other people and her identity. Here mans spirit is always dissatisfied. Sheila's final fate is equal to the view of suicide expounded by Camus in Le Myths de Sisyphe an absurd impossibility of establishing rapport between thing and people. The traditional authorial omniscience is revealed through the direct revelation of actions through the protagonists: they create their lives as they live.

The protagonist's movement in *An Answer from Limbo* and in *I am Mary Dunne* is a discovery that a rigid and vaulting pursuit of a dearly held ambition and base interactions are detrimental to oneself and to the others. Selfish obsessive pursuit to be a writer not only destroys Brending Tierney but all the related ones also. Mary's relations with all men leaves her an empty shell of self. Therefore, as Jo Dunoghue suggests, "it is not in the self or through the self that the greatest fulfilment for self will be found".[17] Naturally we are impelled to that reality other than one self. It can be the intermediary selves of others that do not stultify our image. It points too to that Being, that transcendental search for a spiritual entity that is the cause and final form of our self.

The self and the awareness of itself as victim, the interior monologue that brings the inconsistent ego and its quilt and cinematic style of Sheila's search for an identity are suitable adaptations of technique to variations of themes. In the Belfast Novels, the baffled egos of men beg for a form which transcends empirical reality.

Graham Greene's Joseph Andrews' search for a trust in Elizabeth and Raven's search for point of integrity in the actress all fail. The self's search for certainty and happiness, fails interiorly and exteriorly. Dr. Cziners' sense of justice is baffled, Condor too is dejected in the loss of social sense of justice. All of them are alienated and lost in their patrimonial heritage, ethical code, social structure and above all in their religious practices.

What is shown by Graham Greene as the grappling grim realities of life that contribute to the existential tension of man is elucidated and elaborated by Brian Moore in the protagonists adopted from the Catholic Church, which is noted for its infallibility. Peripheral observation and ritualistic practices, a repressive hegemony under the pretext of education and sexual repression that is constantly considered as normal course where celibacy is a cherished virtue are repeatedly shown in the Belfast Novels of Brian Moore. An attempt to project a fool-proof perfect system to the surrounding Protestants and the consequent prejudiced and hollow interrelations that lay foundation to countless mores as values to human ego, are also described by Brian Moore. All these contribute to the understanding of the protagonists of Graham Greene who are sharing the protestant climate of England and searching for an ego that can do justice to life. Thus "the heart-piercing, reason be-wildering world" of Graham Greene and Brian Moore long for a self-fulfilling, integrating form for the identity of personality.

The first explicit search for a form outside one's own domesticity is portrayed by Brian Moore in *The Temptation of Eileen Hughes*. Bernard McAuleys desertion of priesthood, is not adequately compensated in his wife Mona. His impotency, couples with his failure as a religious, naturally persuade him to look for a beauty that can satisfy his aesthetic ego. Eileen Hughes the salesgirl, her journey to the city and visit of the museum like mansion and Bernard's constant invitation for her family to a palatial mansion in London are all subconscious projections of paternity that long for virility, protection, and the realisation of his own ego Though Eileen Hughes gets an emotional experience in the American youth in the hotel, *The Temptation of Eileen Hughes* is really the temptation of Bernard for that fulfilment outside his domesticity. Thus Moore rings the search for a form through the guise of a female protagonist. This is the act of creating a God.

In the movement of the novel/Bernard's passion to Eileen is religious and devout. He says:

> But having you here, so close, having you all to myself in London, seeing in Kentwood having you say that you wanted to live in a big house, it was too great a temptation (TEH 77).

He loved God. His vocation was rejected and he realized "Gods are like the sun. You can't go too close. They will burn you. Gods do not like you to get cheeky (TEH 59). And therefore he turns to be a maniac of obsession through an empirical reality that takes the place of transcendent.

> "I am trying to save myself, not save the world. I told you, when I was twenty I wanted to be saint, to save my soul, to love God, to do good. But it seems I was not wanted in that way . . . until I met you, until that day I saw you standing in the shop, I never knew what real happiness was (TEH 76).

Thus, the protagonist baptizes him in a quasi-religious attitude for personal fulfilment. In a positive tone Graham Greene too creates champions of justice and spiritual values in his later novels known as the "Catholic Trilogy".

Pinkie of Brighton Rock is another Peter Pan doomed to be juvenile for a life time. Deprived of father and mother in a most cruellest manner and brought-upon a prison-like house, his footing is similar to that of Judith Hearne and all the major premises for lost childhood is served. David Price-Jones comments "If any one deserved to be damned by any moral canons, it is Pinkie yet he has worked to a kind of Sanctity through Rose."[18]

Greene reserves his judgement, and sees through God's eye when he asks who can conceive of "the . . . appalling . . . strangeness of the mercy of God." (BR246) and thus the novel ends as a powerful plea for the victims of the terror of life as an open gestalt of experience. But Pinkie and Raven do not grow up and remain the great champions of Justice.

In the two central characters of *The Power and the Glory*—the wavering priest and the upright officer—the ambiguity of the human situation is brought out. Nauseated both from within and without, the priest has no love for life: "It was sometimes a mistake for life to go on" (PG 169), "He had given way to despair – and out of that had emerged a human soul and love – not the best love, but love all the same (PG 100).

After his final arrest he is troubled by his inadequacy "a few communions, a few confessions, and an endless bad example" (PG 208). On the morning of his execution, "He felt only an immense disappointment because he had to go God empty-handed, with nothing at all. It seemed to him, at that moment, that it would have been quite easy to have been a saint. It would only have needed a little self restraint and a little courage" (PG 210).

Robert A. Witkhert notes that the heroism of the priest is "only through his agony of inadequacy".[19] But David Lodge thinks: "It is the priest's wavering, undignified but persistent loyalty to his vocation that makes him a genuine martyr."[20]

The priest fails, but not the priesthood. The physical plane gets its redemption in the committed dedicated soul of the priest, opening the theological intuitive realisation that there is hope of redemption for a world sunk in amorass of despair, conflict, absurdity and alienation.

In *The Heart of the Matter*, as Graham Greene remarks:

> I had meant the story of Scobie to enlarge a theme which I had already touched on in The Ministry of Fear, the disastrous effect on human beings of pity as distinct from compassion. I had written in The Ministry of Fear 'pity' is cruel, pity destroys. Love is not safe when pity's prowling round.[21]

Scobie's onerous responsibility to save the situation throws him on the horns of a dilemma. He can neither leave Louise nor marry Helen. The sense of protection in him lands him to professional indiscretion and then to corruption, sacrilege and finally suicide. Scobie's individual integrity stands above the collective wisdom of the Church. He is tossed in doubt and faith, affirmation and denial, and he never finds a full stop to his faith.

The over-riding factor that permeates these early novels as well as the Catholic trilogy is that all of them recognize the reality of evil as a basic factor of human life. Good and evil are treated both as human and Catholic problems. In *The Heart of the Matter*, for example, when Louise puts Scobie to a religious test, it is all "honey" to Helen. After Scobie's death Louise seeks theological help and Helen's search does not have a prop. The perusers are transcending from the realm of "loyalty" and "disloyalty" to the question "Is Scobie damned?" But Greene writes:

> May be I am too harsh to the book, wearied as I have been by reiterated arguments in Catholic journals on Scobie's salvation or damnation. I was not so stupid as to believe that this could ever be an issue in a novel. Besides I have small belief in the doctrine of eternal punishment (it was Scobie's belief, not mine). (WE 120).

But it is obvious that Pinkie is sent to hell and the whisky priest to heaven and Scobie to purgatory. The question that begs to save our mind from perplexity is the mystery of God's grace. Thus, the fundamental question posed in the "Catholic Trilogy" is salvation through grace; and the escathological dimension of life. What is achieved by Greene is commented upon by Terry Eagleton:

> Orthodoxy is submitted to the test of experience and its inadequacies exposed: but not to the point where it might be shown up as hollow - revealed for instance as bad theology - for that would be to slacken the tension between orthodoxy and humanity, and so to

destroy the guilty self disgust by which the believer is rendered superior to the rationalist."[22]

Without exception, Greene's novels are permeated with squalor, corruption, guilt and betrayal, crime, violence death and defeat. To come to terms with life, the heros and heroines critically consider the choices before them.

The End of the Affair gives an account of human love with the entwined passions of jealously and hatred further fanned by the unexpected intrusion of divine love. Critics are of the opinion that none of the religious novels of Graham Greene takes escatholical preoccupation manifestly as it is in *The End of the Affair*. Anna Freemantle says:

> Greene preeminently builds his stories with ends, not means . . . death is not merely a period, a full stop. Always present in all his books, it is sometimes a goal, a consummation devoutly wished, . . . and inevitably, it is an event of more than private or physical significance."[23]

In his concern with the cessation of existence Pinkie is doomed hell, the whisky priest is in heaven, and scobie, despite grievous sin, is on his way to salvation. Sarah Miles in *The End of the Affair* like Mary Magdalin and St. Augustine, is led from concupiscence to sanctification.

Greene's experience of the religious and the faithful is bleak and cruel. The sea of faith for him is a 'cruel sea'. He writes in *Ways of Escape*.

> This account may seem cynical and unfeeling, but in the years between *The Heart of the Matter* and *The End of the Affair* I felt myself used and exhausted by the victims of religion. The vision of faith as an untroubled sea was lost for ever; faith was more like a tempest in which the lucky were engulfed and lost, and the unfortunate survived to be flung battered and bleeding on the shore. (WE 253)

In *The End of the Affair*, Sarah is lucky to be engulfed and lost and Bendrix, though at a safe distance from the tempest's fury, is one of those left battered and bleeding on the shore. The plot is basically about adultery and remorse. Whatever else Sarah is, she is a fallen women. She turns her back on that state of moral guilt with extraordinary determination and agony of mind, and returns to her husband.

If Sarah triumphs in anything it seems precisely to be in her will to give up Bendrix. And thus the moral order is affirmed and restored. But contrary to this, Marie Davenport of Brian Moore's Cold Heaven, is caught up in an "amoral indifference" and continue sot persist in it without a mark of redemption.

The difference in the mental set up of these women protagonists has to be probed into. The main reason that stands out is that the antithesis or the opposite masculine energy both of them shares is varied. Bendrix is an embodiment of hatred and jealousy, whereas Marie's partner is a doctor in research more caught up in the aura of research and medicinal practice than in Marie. Sarah has caught up in the eros of the two getting dejected at the brink of the death of her lover at her very nose. Marie's eros is emanating from a secular framework and not get shuddered. For from the tragedy of her husband he gets miraculous escape in the same swiftness as the miracle enters in her life. She too escapes out of a suspicion that her hiding of the revelation is the cause of the tragedy of Davenport. Thus when the previous order is revoked the mind is let loose of its Eros and now the natural vent is Alex. All forces against this union is counted as alienating.

Bendrix's entry into Sarah's life indifferent from that of Marie's extramarital affair. On a wet January night in 1946, Bendrix has a chance encounter with Henry Miles, Sarah's husband. Bendrix, the middle-aged novelist and Sarah, the wife of Henry - a senior civil servant, are lovers. Eighteen months have passed since Sarah and Bendrix met. Their 'affair', lasting through most of the war, runs an uneven passionate and unscrupulous course, largely owing to the tormented jealousy, bitterness and hatred of Bendrix. It is brought to an abrupt end during an air raid. Bendrix is knocked unconscious under a door. After a few minutes he recovers, goes upstairs, and finds Sarah on her knees praying. She leaves the house and he does not see her again. All his attempts to get in to contact with her fail. So Bendrix's jealousy flames up again when Henry tells him that he suspects Sarah of unfaithfulness, for she is often absent in the house. Hearing this and taking the intention of Henry for private enquiry, Bendrix employs (without Henry's a knowledge, Parkins) an inept and slightly grotesque private detective, to follow Sarah's movements. The detective steals Sarah's diary from which Bendrix learns the truth about Sarah's conduct. During the air-raid, Sarah, believing Bendrix to be dead, had made a bargain with God promising that she would give Bendrix up, if He would restore him to life. She tries, in vain, various ways of forgetting him. She visits a rationalist preacher, hoping that he will convince her to break her bargain. But his arguments only feed her faith. Her love for Bendrix continues as strongly as ever, and in the closing entries of her diary, she begs God for peace. She, all human loving surpassing, has "caught belief like a disease" and before Maurice can bring her back to human love, she dies of pneumonia. After her death and though her intervention, the private detective's little boy is cured of appendicitis and the rationalist preacher of a strawberry mark. Invited by Henry, Bendrix goes to share his house, his jealousy and hatred of Sarah's lover unabated by the fact that his rival was not human but divine.

By introducing a miracle, does Greene have a didactic axe to grind? Of course are strong suggestions which imply Sarah's sanctity and healing through her intervention, but it is left to the reader's imagination to make what they want of these suggestions, because there is sufficient evidence against the sanctity of the heroine. In her journal Sarah had written: You are too good to me, when I ask you for pain, you give me peace. Give it to him too. Give him my peace, he needs it more" (EA 123). Bendrix comments after her death:

> We could all be saints by leaping as you leapt, by shutting the eyes and leaping once and for all . . . It's something he can demand of any of us . . . But I won't leap . . . you're a devil, God, tempting us to leap. But I don't want your peace and I don't want your love . . . I hate you, God, I hate you as though you existed (EA 190-91).

So Bendrix's reaction to Sarah's leap and the sanctity thrust upon her do not cement the notion of the novel as a plea for sainthood via adultery. Regarding the miracle too we have to avoid the rational explanation of by Bendrix. The first in the series is Bendrix coming alive after the bomb explosion. It is a sheer coincidence that Bendrix who is knocked unconscious for a few minutes should be presumed dead by Sarah. Sarah herself ascribes her delusion in presuming Bendrix dead and her bargain with God to a moment of hysteria: only she cannot break that vow. She is not sure whether her private pact with God counts or not. But this miracle transports her soul to a higher plane of faith and leads to family loyalty. This transforming power of miracle is absent in Cold Heaven.

The healing of Parkin's boy and the disappearance of Smythe's mulberry mark keep the novel always in the theological atmosphere. Where as in Cold Heaven the guilt begetted by the hiding up of a divine revelation and the psychological endeavour to execute the demand of the miracle sustain the divine element in the novel.

Since these miracles do not take place in the strict ecclesiastical context, they do not fulfil the canonical criteria of a religious miracle. But even in the secular context they have a function in the novel—to elicit our attitude towards miracles and to bring in grace even in the most despicable human situation. The abundance of divine mercy and the fact that nothing is impossible to God is reiterated. As *Holy Bible* says, it is "not on our merit but on His Grace" that things depend.

The technique that Greene employs to elicit the readers' response is masterly. When Graham Greene commences the novel from the paradoxical statement: "A story has no beginning or end; arbitrarily one chooses that moment of experience from which to look back or from which to look ahead" (EA 7) we yearn for that moment of experience that the novel can provide; and grist is added to the mill of our curiosity. Again our imagination is taken up by the lonely sight of Henry Miles slanting across the wide river of rain on a January night on the common with reveries of hate towards Henry.

Thus, at the very outset we are made to suspend our ideas and ponder on that man who slants down; we are baffled by the mystery of "that evening". Even then we are compelled to think in the same tenor in the face of the bold statement, "So this is a record of hate fare more than of love" and we are teased to curiosity, we are impelled to follow effortlessly Bendrix, from whose view point the major portion of the novel is narrated.

Our imagination reverts to the past in technique, and we are compelled to come back to the present when we share Henry's worry about Sarah's demeanour. Thus, from the curiosity of a novelist, Bendrix comes to reality; "of course it's possible, Sarah's human." But Bendrix is mired in a Cauldron of hate and suspicion.

Sarah is warned at first, ". . . you are wet through, Sarah one day you will catch your death of cold," and when in reality it occurs at the end of the novel, we become agitated and excited to the thematic as well as structural gestalt of the novel.

The *End of the Affair becomes* 'a medium to think with' in the ruminations of Bendrix. Hatred seems to operate the same glance as love: it even produces the same actions.

> If we had not been taught how to interpret the story of passion, would we have been able to say from their actions alone whether it was the jealous Judas or the cowardly Peter who loved Christ (EA 21).

The lunch that Mrs. Hiles hoisted is the consummate moment in which Bendrix's ego is presented to us. The Callous indifference of Bendrix to marital love is brought out; "but I remember nothing else, how Sarah looked the first time or what we did, except that we were both nervous and made love badly. It didn't matter. We had started, that was the point" (EA 45).

By interpolating this love with a curious personal philosophy such as: "The act of love itself has been described as the little death, and lovers sometimes experience the little peace" (EA 47) the author takes us to a new tenet of personal thinking that permeates our interpersonal relationship. Bendrix believes that "distrust grows with lovers success" (EA 48); on the other hand Sarah confesses, "I have never loved anybody or anything as I do you" (EA 48). In her complete abandonment, she transcends time and space to be part of eternity. Thus Graham Greene, through the opposite poles of love, leads the reader to a transcendence that has its root on earth. "Facticity" is adeptly transcended in the most intimate moment of human relationship to give the reader's mind a space above matter. The lines:

> "when I replied that I loved her too in that way, I was a liar not she, for I never lose the consciousness of time: to one the present is never here: It is always last year or next week." He adds "Even in moment of love I was like a police officer gathering evidence of a crime that hadn't yet been committed. . ." (EA 51)

The entrapped love and suspicion which one finds the self-abandonment of perfect love and self-assertion of a possessive sort are the appropriate atmosphere to analyse the diary discovered by Parkis. A progress in the perusal of Sarah's diary is a progress in the realisation of the process and stages of Sarah's conversion.

The crisis when Bendrix is thrashed into rubble by the ravage of the raid, Sarah has a faint concept of God and prays to "anything that might exist (EA 88). Then she resolves to be loyal in her conjugal love. Thus crisis purges herself, prunes her attitude and forms her character to be upright in life and to be in constant touch with God. Bendrix's bitterness and hatred against Henry Miles increases who happens to be the glorious husband of a saint. Thus bitterness and hatred assumes a colour of divinity and look askance at the conversion and sainthood. This superb touch on the peruser's creative imagination is really challenging.

From a shaky floor of faith, Sarah comes to a secular look into life to entice the reader to an endearment to a mere mundane life. At one moment of deep aridity that scathes the very narrow of bones he says: "He (God) cannot exist, you can't have a merciful God and this despair" (EA 93) It is from lack of faith and marital disloyalty we are taken to conversion and sainthood. This is the divine realm we are led to.

In *The End of the Affair* the sumptuous lunch hosted to the newspaper journalist and the later bomb raid is the background against with the betrayal and discernment of divinity enter in the life of Sarah Miles. Whereas the picnic and boating by a researcher are the background in which the guilt of an unexpressed apparition of the real husband are portrayed. But Brian Moore takes a unique course of events to elucidate the process of the loss of faith in individuals. The Church's collective inquisition on the divine moments of human psyche may isolate the individual and may sever his relation with Church and its faith. This may in turn increase the momentum of disloyalty in conjugal love.

The guilt that Marie feels at the time of the accident of her husband obviously betrays the delicacy of her personality. Similar are the feelings of Sarah Miles at the spot of Bendrix's accident. Marie feels: "Something bad, an accident happened to this person. I know something that makes me believe. Being punished for not telling what I saw" (CH 123). To free her of this guilt of omission, she approaches Monsignor Cassidy – "the god's golfer." Though Cassidy gives a tenable secular and relaxing approach to the situation, Father Ned Niles' presence annonys Alex when he returns from Moffit Hospital.

The apparition finds a new owner in sister Anna's assertion of the vision of Saint Marg. Marie uses this opportunity to change her stand. She says: "I saw nothing. I did not believe in those days. I do not want to believe in them . . . A person has a right not to believe (CH 267). Thus here the decision to desert faith—the food of the Soul—gets its upper hand and the possibility of loyalty in family is left asundered. Sarah Miles finds her conversion and grace in crisis, but in the very context of Church Marie finds a lot of faith. And she corrupts incorrigibly by sharing bed with Daniel. Loss of faith and loss of love run hand in hand in Cold Heaven. Still the theological aura is kept in the persons of sister Mother St. Jude and Anna.

The rejected miracle has given a respite, "a silence". But in that moment too she doesn't get enlightened. Marie describes the entire episode as follows. Like a battlefield it had become its history, its truth altered to fit the legend of those who had survived she thought of David, who would never know about this, of Alex who had been part of it without knowing.

An unshared miracle, an unshared belief – yes, a transcendental theological experience and energy to "remember in silence for the rest of her life", yet happy to be with "that ordinary, muddled life of falling in love and leaving her husband and starting over again," that is the puzzle the modern consciousness confronts when the Church forms a gang of inquisitors searching for the veracity. Scrutinising the faith experience of one may lead to a refusal of public admission of it, though in the core of the heart a person would "remember it in silence for the rest of her life." The existential guilt that is transmitted to us through the corporate personality of Adam and Eve at last succumbs us to submit, though a beacon of light is stored and shined in the mystical body of the Church. In the inexplicable self-absorption and introspection modern mind does not allow itself to be scrutinized and externalised and continue in harmony with a mere ordinary life. Faith through miracle as a structure or a phenomenon standing outside as an added reality is despised; but faith that lives in soul, though disloyalty rules the daily mode of life seems to be the apparent theme of the novel. Though guilty and sinful due to the tragic predicament of life, man can be essentially innocent and open to God. Just like Graham Greene is very eloquent in Brighton Rock about this tenet of thinking, Brian Moore too argues it here. Thus the riddle of faith and freedom is getting its practical explanations and pragmatic difficulties in the novels of Graham Greene and Brian Moore. Faith that transcends the existential disloyalty culminating in miracle after death is the theme of *The End of the Affairs* too.

Even with all the personal love, spiritual association, and miracle, Marie is lost in flesh whereas Sarah achieves sainthood. The freedom to believe or not to believe fuses in them. Sarah believes but Marie is not believing. This theme in Cold Heaven, is boldly attempted, contrasting the secular and the religious. Brian Moore narrates the inspiration on this attempt thus:

> Years ago, I started writing something concerning carmel, became afraid and backed off. Two years ago,

> while visiting my sister who belongs to an order of catholic working nuns in England, I was struck by what I sense is true holiness. . . . "I was impressed with the sanctity in some of the older nuns – a feeling that mystics had; they had no sense of self, souls and solum in God. I corresponded with them about what they really felt; but I didn't have the intellectual capability or perhaps the religious capability to write about it.[24]

He accepted and admired their faith. But Maries Davenport develops a claustrophobia "To shut oneself away from the world, alone with God, she felt a panicky impulse to open the door and run out of the convent (CH, 224). Thus the novel keeps its distance from the author.

But the insufficiency and inferiority of an institutionalised faith represented in a group of inquisitors by Brian Moore and in a rationalist preacher by Graham Greene against the background of Sinners and half or non-believers like Sarah and Marie are rightly contrasted and prepares us sympathetically for an urge to the supernatural.

In the essay, "Brian Moore's Fiction of Faith", Michael Paul Gallagher has made a serious attempt to detect and elaborate on a consistent theme of faith in the whole of Moore's work in the thirty years since the publication of Judith Hearne up to and including Black Robe, As Gallagher remarks,

> "The expansion of faith theme from literal or narrowly religious world into a metaphysical metaphor is the main topic of this article"[25]

Yet it appears that in *Cold Heaven* the "faith theme" has both a literal and metaphorical resonance in it. Is not this a novel with transcendental or supernatural theme? The Cote d' Azur is going to be transformed into the coast of California for much of the novel, but despite the commercialisation of the first and the relative inaccessibility of the second, there is much in common between them and this is emphasized here. In the opening sentence, the helplessness of the individual faced with great cosmic forces is expressed. The seats of the "little" pedal boat, the "little" underlying vulnerability, "force" Marie to look up. The sky is not hostile or threatening but "vast" and "clear". The movement into danger, a danger which Marie realizes only at the end of the novel, is signified by their passage into the "deeper, more solitary waters of the Baie des Anges". With great economy the author prepares us for the fatal accident. Relationship between Alex and Marie it is depicted at first they paddled in union', but very soon their disharmony is signalled by the difference in their efforts. Marie slackened her efforts but Alex continued determinedly. Their first words of communication are words of disagreement, her remarks suggestive and conciliatory, his "I want" assertive and even dogmatic.

From our recognition of Marie as the protagonist in the first few sentences, with the free and indirect speech of the second paragraph, the reader is invited into the central consciousness and voice of the novel. Her decision to "leave him" prods us to conclude that they are husband and wife. In the short even sentences a different mental process is conveyed: observation, memory reaches at a decision which postpones the decision to tell she thus appears to be in a position of power; she knows something that Alex does not; yet she is powerless to act upon her decision. These paragraphs have a value as an opening passage of introspection before the period of frenzied activity which begins, not just when the launch hits Alex, but when Alex begins to swim in an energetic and erratic free-style.

Marie is presented in a relationship that lacks all credibility. Her disillusion is emphasized. But there is no sympathy for Alex. Yet her powerlessness also emerges. She is Alex's victim now, as she will be his hostage later on and also the victim of other, more powerful forces. She has no power because she lacks all courage; in this she is contrasted with Mother St. Jude who has none of Marie's obvious intellectual or material advantages yet has tremendous spiritual power. Thus, a protagonist who is baffled by internal powerlessness and who counts even a supernatural apparition as an addition to her existential internal impotency: She treats everything as 'other powers' to victimize her. Thus, the radical helplessness of the individual surrounded by baffling forces both secular and divine; In this lethargic state of mind initiative is destroyed and the mind remains cold to the external world.

Thus in the consciousness of victimisation, fear pervades, spontaneity is marred, ego is lost in the warring factions, and harmony with the more essential and vital part of nature (humanity) is hampered. In her marital relationship with Alex, who has scholarly bent in the field of medicine, she might have felt victimised, Naturally she longs for spontaneity and affection from other sources. The novelist and Sarah in *The End of the Affair* too face the same situation.

Brian Moore deliberately sustains the response of the reader and the virtual dimension of the reality presented at the opening paragraph, and tries to keep it till the end. The closing paragraph of the novel is:

> She looked up at the sky. No guns were trained from on high, ready to shoot her down. . . . She thought of that life, that ordinary, muddled life of falling in love and leaving her husband and starting over again that known and imperfect existence that she had fought to regain against ineluctable forces, inexplicable odds . . . She looked up toward the point Lobos Motor Inn. She began to walk toward's Alex's unit, rehearsing what she would say to him (CH 270-71).

Unlike the opening sentence, the sky is clouded. In the extended and elaborate similes of the next two sentences, the relief Marie feels at her deliverance from the supernatural forces that threaten to engulf her, is highlighted. These images are "given" to Marie, framed as they are between the two sentences, "she looked up at the sky" and "she thought of Daniel".

In this paragraph, existence, not just life, is postulated in opposition to the essential and the incomprehensible "ineluctable forces, inexplicable odds". The use of the word "ineluctable" is apparently paradoxical. Marie chooses to fight and not to yield to these forces so far as belief is concerned. She sees herself several times, as being forces to negotiate to do things and to go places against her will and she is released from these obligations only by the grace and favour of the Church. Her victory and her loss are conveyed simultaneously, both in the banal statement of "ordinary muddled life" and in a more thoughtful and philosophical phrase "that known and imperfect existence". The victory of every day life is gained at the expense of the transcendent; "the mundane over the metaphysical, empirical over the metempirical. In the imperfect existence she is a battlefield.

Marie is a split personality who is torn between Alex and Daniel. By mere coincidence she finds a religious anchorage in an apparition. Had it been welcomed and ratified and proceeded on, it would have been a successful experience that would have shaped Maries personality till the end, leading her to be a champion of a superego that is expressed in concrete facts. But that ego and experience are kept in abeyance and investigated and raked upon by so many in the form of an inquisition; leading to the loss of the sublimation of personality. It can happen and it does happen in *Cold Heaven*. Prayer does not supplement the event of miracle and no conversion takes place. The malady of the husband makes Marie remember the apparition she had; but she does not pray as Sarah does, but rushes to testify to the church. Her purpose is not to surrender but to avoid a guilt and to get a shape to her guilty ego. St. Paul has said "Faith without deeds is dead" and that is verified here. A secular ego sans contact with God through prayer may eschew the opportunity for conversion. If Marie happens to be such a case, Graham Greene's Sarah (*The End of the Affair*) is just the reverse of it. Here is study in parallel and contrast in the field of faith.

When we compare and contrast *The End of the Affair* with *Cold Heaven*, both the novels are akin in depicting the absurdity of human situations and the existential tension of being a modern man. The predicaments of the protagonists in both the novels are equal. In terms of the German existentialist Heidegger the "encompassing" environment that both Sarah and Marie Devanport face seems to be are hostile to their growth as integrated personalities. As beings, they too are "in-itself" in scholastic terminology, they are "supposits". But as Sartre says, they must be "for-itself"- too. Thus, the existential tension of "in-itself" and "for-itself" confronts an encompassing environment which is equally divided. Sarah is the target of hatred and jealousy and is in agony of violated loyalty, which seeks a time to recede to its origin. The "tension' is of the old conflict between "loyalty" and "disloyalty". The Church, particularly the Catholic church is simply, a catalyst, to form an attitude, a conversion.

Marie Davenport counts the non disclosure of a divine apparition of St. Mary as the cause of the tragedy of her husband. But she does not surrender herself to be possessed by religion. So the miracle is just a moment to find form- an identity of the mind and when it is gained she falls back to the lap of flesh. In the case of Sarah it is a return to purity, but in Marie Davenport, even with a divine silence and energy in mind, it is ending in alienation. Thus each one find the fulfilment of the "in-itself" and the extraneous relation to the other masculine energy—one of the essential element "for-itself"—in a particular way singular to each one. Marie does not follow external criteria as the liberator of her being, when she counts the ecclesiastical officers as an inimical block.

Sarah leaps to a faith at the moment of her lover's peril and takes a decision in front of a "God" who has no external formulation in a particular church From the angle of faith, we are left with the question 'what type of faith is it?' God reached down into Sarah's private hell of lust and adultery and she like the whisky-priest, succumbed to Him.

Sarah's acts of faith is represented as one of those irrational act (Sarah herself recognizes itself as 'hysteria') which appears out of character. Characters like the whisky-priest, Scobie and Sarah are driven by instincts of which they may be only half aware or not aware at all. It always becomes, an irrecoverable and irreconcilable act, and from this original act emanate consequences which eventually entrammel the agent and bring about his spiritual or physical death, or both.

A striking parallel to Sarah's faith is provided in Graham Greene's play *The Potting Shed* in the prayer of Father William Callifer. He offers to God what he loves most, (his faith), in return for his nephew James' life. James who had hanged himself in the shed lies seemingly lifeless, and when he comes back to life, the priest thinks his prayer has been answered. For him it is the beginning of the agony of being without God. Sarah and Father Callifer struggle painfully against the consequences of their prayers—the imposition of new identities.

This irrational act of faith in Sarah and the faith of Marie in *Cold Heaven* which come to her in an apparition but not preventing her back from going to her lover can, be termed in the terminology of Jean-Paul-Sartre as "bad faith"[26] For here, the dreaded unconscious forces of id and libido have an upper hand over rationality and decision based on reason. Thus both the novels testify that existence gets its success and precedence over essence. But later Marie has a "silence" to carry with her wherever she goes and Sarah has a conversion which ends in miracle even after death. Thus, even in our bad faith we are not left alone. God seems to be an unseen presence—the third in their life's journey to Emmaus. Sarah feels that in loving Bendrix she has loved God all the time and that the act of love has always implied an act of faith; reminding us of Coleridge's dictum, "He prayeth well, who loveth well".[27]

In both the novels faith seems to be the anchorage or configuration on which the existential tension between "in-itself" and "for-itself", converge. Bad faith can be a stepping stone to good faith. Both novelists fight against an unpronounced feeling or sometimes at least a vein of thinking of the human mind that God does not work among the sinners. But the fornication of Sarah and the disloyalty of Marie are treated from the point of view of redemption and sainthood. This gives us a "new vein of thinking"[28] a right type of thinking.

The psyche process in bad faith is substantiated by Sartre as:

> "The human being is not only the being by whom negatives are disclosed in the world, he is also the one who can take negative attitudes with respect to himself. Consciousness is a being the nature of which is to be conscious of the nothingness of its being.[29]

Our consciousness is not restricted to envisioning a negative. It constitutes itself in its own flesh as the inhalation of a possibility. For that reason it must arise in the world as a No. It is as a "No" that the slave first apprehends the master, and the prisoner who tries trying to escape sees the guard who watches him. There are even men whose social reality is uniquely that of No, who will live and die. This is elucidated by Marie Davenport. What are we to say about the being of a man who has the possibility of denying himself. And Sartre concludes:

> It is best to choose and to examine one determined attitude which is essential to human reality and which

> is such that consciousness instead of directing its negation outward turns it toward itself. This attitude, it seems to be, is bad faith. . . . To be sure, the one who practices bad faith is hiding a displeasing truth or presenting as truth a pleasing untruth. The duality of the deceiver and the deceived does not exist here. Bad faith on the contrary implies in essence the unity of a single consciousness.[30]

While discussing the patterns of bad faith, Sartre very clearly brings forth the situations through which the protagonists pass when the divorce of the body from the soul occurs with the lascivious paramours neither consenting nor resisting the act of love it, is a case of bad faith.

From bad faith, the art of forming contradictory concepts which unite in themselves both an idea and the negation of that idea, the double property of the human being, namely, facticity and transcendence, are engendered.

> The two aspects of human reality are and ought to be capable of a bold co-ordination. But bad faith seeks to affirm their identity while preserving their differences. It just affirm facticity as being transcendence and transcendence as being facticity in such a way that at the instant when a person apprehends the one, he finds himself abruptly faced with the other.[31]

In these novels we face human reality "as a being which is what it is not and which is not what it is".[32] To be sincere is to be what one is. That supposes that I am not originally what I am. I can become sincere, this is what my duty and effort to achieve sincerity imply. In bad faith human reality is constituted as a being which is what it is not and which is not what it is."

The misunderstood facticity and transcendence is the cog around which characters like Bendrix, Henry and Sarah as spokes of a wheel revolves. Bendrix is full of hatred and possessives love and refuses to leap'. Henry is suspicious and searches for a spy to verify his thesis form the life data of Sarah. In the marital bond he cannot transcend and sublimate his suspicion. Sarah, even after the miraculous escape of her lover, yearns for the "Corrupt love" of Bendrix.

In *Cold Heaven*, Brian Moore's protagonist's too reveal an utter lack of sincerity and a misunderstand of facticity and transcendence. Marie Davenport takes all the opportunity of rid of Alex and counts choice of Daniel as a sincere one. The apparition results only in forming an inimical block. No time is left to rectify and manumit herself from the tragic clutches of bad faith. Marie is contrasted with the holy love of Mother St. Jude, and the Monsignor. But even then she follows the flaw of her will. From a mystical point of view Marie and Sarah occupy different realms. Marie's experience of a dynamic external presence—described classically in Rudolf Otto's *The Idea of the Holy* as that of a "mysterium", "tremendum" and "fascinatum"—an awe-inspiring fascinating mystery she has immediate contact with the transcendent in the apparition of producing the Holy Mother. But it is not an introvertive mysticism.

For W.T. Stale speaks "introvertive mysticism, "the characteristics of which are an experience which is somehow timeless, it gives the mystic bliss and an apprehension of the transcendent which accrues upon a course of self-mastery and contemplation."[33] But in *Mysticism Sacred and Profane* R.C. Zachner talks of "extrovertive mysticism"[34] where one gains a rapport with the world. It has no prophetic function. Thus, Marie in her revelation finds an accidental explanation of the tragedy of her husband but her future life is unaffected. Sarah uses the tragedy of the second lover to achieve a rapport with the first one. Thus, both of them are in the grip of an extrovertive mysticism.

As for a classical analysis, of love: in Homer it appears as "Eros" and it is simply a common noun meaning "love" or "desire". In Hesiod's *Theogony* "Eros" becomes one of the three primordial Gods and has no offspring. Yet it outgrows differences, limits and overcomes the reason of both men and gods. When Aphrodite is born from the sperm of Granu's, Eros accompanies her into the council of gods. Later through Empedocles the idea of cycles was introduced and world history was placed as an alternative of the "Love and Strife" – the principle of composition and decomposition, of disintegration. Thus, sexual love becomes one example of the universal power of union. It provides us with empirical evidence of a metaphysical principle. In Christianity, it is essential. God's love seems to be thought of as subject to volition. Thus belief becomes a source of understanding. Later, great emphasis was given to ceremonies and expressions, of devotion, and the greatest moment was the Christian agape in which the devout is meant to share a supper and to rejoice in their common belief. The transformation expected from this source of common belief is a life of absolute trust and absolute love. Life should be a trust in love and love in trust. The capacity of a person for this life, even after a fall, is verified in Sarah's will. The incapacity for this life in its process and possibility is explicated in Maries weak flesh.

Sarah's love is transformed from Eros through Strife to Agape. But Marie's love still remains in the subconscious dimension of "Eros". Why is this? Is it because of her purely secular frame of mind? Or because of the tragic flaw of the will that is steeped in lust and selfishness? The unbridled expression of a secular instinct in its spontaneity may loses sight of a rationality as in the case of Henchard in Mayor of casterbridge.

The powerful "force of habit" manifested in bad faith. Annihilates the grace of God and the metaphysical freedom of man in *Cold Heaven*. Whereas in Greene, miracle and the world of God annihilates, force of habit and achieve and maintain a conversion and escathological perfection. In this world of 'willing' suspension of belief, disbelief, belief, half-belief and non-belief, people are brought to investigate the theological question "Salvation through grace" or "Salvation through faith"? In *The End of the Affair* Greene exposes the ability of the spirit to enter into salvation relegating the flesh, whereas in Cold Heaven, Moore explicates the inability of the Soul to rise above concupiscence for a life in faith.

NOTES

1. John Wilson Foster, *Question and Answer with Brian Moore*, Irish Literary Supplement 3 (Fall 1985) 44-45.
2. Graham Greene, *The Lost Childhood and other Essays* (London: Penguin, 1962) 76.
3. Brian Moore in *Conversation with Andy O' Mahoney* (RTE Radio 'Dialogue' Feb. 20, 1986).
4. Samuel Hynes, (ed.) *A Collection of Critical Essays, Twentieth Century Views* (New Jersey: Prentice-Hall, 1973) 25.
5. David Lodge. *The Novelist at the Crossroads* (London: Routledge, 1971) 99-100.
6. J. O' Donoghue. *Brian Moore: A Critical Study* (Montreal: MacGill Queens UP, 1991) 37.
7. *Ibid*, 38.
8. Robert Sullivan, "Brian Moore: A Clinging Climate", (*London Magazine* 15 Jan. 1977) 63.
9. Donoghue, *op. cit.*, 17-18.
10. *Ibid*, 27.
11. Jenny Flood. *Brian Moore* (Lewisburg. Bucknell UP, 1974) 13.
12. Donoghue, *op. cit.*, 51.
13. Seamus Deane. *A Short History of Irish Literature* (London: Huchinson, 1986) 220.
14. Graham Greene. *Stamboul Train* (1932, Harmondsworth: Penguin, 1977) 200. Further references to this edition will be indicated in the text by the abbreviation ST followed by page number.
15. Pryce-Jones. *Graham Greene*, (London: Oliver and Boyd, 1966)10.
16. Donoghue, *op.cit.*, 75.
17. *Ibid*, 131.
18. Pryce-Jones, *op.cit.*, 34.

19. Robert A Witkhert. "The quality of Graham Greene's Mercy", (*College English* 25.2 (Nov. 1963) 103.
20. David Lodge, *op.cit.*, 103.
21. Graham Greene, *Ways of Escape* (1981, Harmondsworth: Penguin, 1982) 93: Further reference to this edition will be indicated in the text by the abbreviation WE followed by page number.
22. Terry Eagleton, *Exiles and Eimgres* (London: Chatto and Windus, 1920) 112.
23. Francis Wyndham, *Graham Greene* (British Council Publication, 1962) 32.
24. Mcihael Paul Gallagher, *Brian Moore's Fiction of Faith* (Gaeliana 5, 1985) 92.
25. Michael Paul Gallager, rev. of Cold Heaven, *Irish University Review*. Vol. 14, 1984. pp-31-34.
26. Jean-Paul Sartre. *Being and Nothingness*, (New York, Washington Square, 1980) 86.
27. R.C. Sharma, *A Stucy on 'The Rime of Ancient Mariner* (Delhi: Aarti Book Centre, 1967) 71.
28. Sethuraman, 265.
29. Jean-Paul Sartre, *op.cit.*, 86.
30. Sartre, *op.cit.*, 89.
31. *Ibid*, 98.
32. *Ibid*, 101.
33. W.T. Stale, *The Encyclopedia of Pholosphy*, Vol.8 Mysticism and Philosophy (New York: Collier Macmillan. 1972) 60.
34. R.C. Zachner, *The Encyclopedia of Philosophy*. Vol. 8, Mysticism Sared and profane, 81.

5 ZEST - THE FLAVOUR OF LIFE

In the lethargic flight of modern life, many men cherish a "death-in-life" and many others experience a life-in-death. The scorching, blistering rays of modern life find exponents of a 'death of God' as well as "an eclipse of God" both in the philosophical and theological phases of life. W.B. Yeats seems to have felt this loss of the harmony of life adversely, when he wrote:

Things fall apart; the Centre cannot hold;
Mere Anarchy is loosed upon the world,
The blood-dimmed tide is loosed and everywhere
The ceremony of innocence is drowned
The best lack all conviction, while the worst
Are full of passionate intensity.[1]

But there have been conscious efforts to bring out the harmony of life. Theilhard de Chardin sought the "Within" and "Without" of things, for a megasynthesis in a christogenesis. Sigmund Freud tried to create the "Wholeness" of the individual and Carl Jung tried to demythologise man to bring him in to contact with the right reason of life. Literary persons like James Joyce and Virginia Woolf expressed life experiences freed from the rigidity of expression, expressed the stream-of-consciousness technique. T.S. Eliot hunted after new myths and mythical figures that could express the exhaustiveness of life through his objective co-relatives. Graham Greene and Brian Moore in their fictions have tried to bring back the religious sense and the dignity of man in the arena of life. The protagonists of both the novelists feel an inadequacy. After many a tussle most of them escape into a religious dimensions for a fresh start in life and those who are devoured by the scathing tides of life find a vindication in their soul-life in communion with divine grace and mercy.

A survey of the novels of Graham Greene and Brian Moore reveal the fact that both the writers create protagonists who share a zest for life either in an amorphous misdirected manner leading them to "a substitute gratification"; or for a secular or religious cause.

The earlier novels of Graham Greene and Brian Moore verify the negative dimensions of the flavour of life. The central character of *The Man Within*, the first of Greene's novels, Andrews is a "sort of Judas" (MW 63). Existence gets its precedence over his soul. But he is more sinned against than sinning. He has betrayed his only friend Carlyon and taken shelter in Elizabeth's cottage soliloquizing in his panic and fatigued temper, "Dangerous, Dangerous.' But 'a wave of self-pity passed across his mind and he saw himself friendless and alone, chased by harsh enemies through an uninterested world." (MW 24). Andrews, after the betrayal of his friend, is a man of despair. He longs for compassion, concern and understanding. He tells: ". . . all I want is a little sympathy." (MW 24). But as time passes the guilt of his split personality only increases. His mind becomes the arena of a conflict between the ideal, critical superego and the desiring, sentimental child. Out of this internal conflict emerges suspicion of all those who are around him. When he loses his belief in others he began to dread even their glances. Then sense of loneliness cramps his soul: "Loneliness and fear were like emptiness of hunger to his belly (MW 40). Thus, the within of Andrew has no firm ground to stand on.

There is nothing in his soul to give him an impetus to life. Thus, despair, fear and dread at last give place to a maladic indecision. The moment he makes a manly decision, the internal man taunts him, "you are not a man" (MW 60). Thus Andrew's incapacity to take any deliberate human decision comes from the lack of a point of zest in his soul that could lead a person fearlessly at any moment of crisis.

This self-effacement, this absence of self-image, is the meeting ground of Andrews and Elizabeth. It is the man within us which determines our external relations and fruitful interactions. The epigraph from Thomas Browne reflects the internal Andrew: "There's another man within me that's angry with me." (MW 6).

The helpless Andrews is a 'determined' personality like that of Judith in Brian Moore's first novel. The present moment is not under his control. Andrews is a hunted man. He is being pursued by the smugglers whom he has betrayed to the law. And the past, too did not favour him. He blames his father for his cowardice and irresolution. "My father and mother made me. I didn't make myself" (MW 52). "But his father was a mountain and how could he bring forth such a mouse" (MW 71). To prove his importance, he betrays his friends to the law and now he got the stigma of "a Sort of Judas" (MW, 63). The absence of an internal point of fervor makes him empty. In the quite recline of Elizabeth, he finds some peace. In the quite recline of Elizabeth, he finds some peace. She emerges a paragon of pristine beauty and love. It is at the instigation of Elizabeth that he prepares to go to Lewes and bear witness against smugglers. But there he meets the prosecutors' mistress Lucy. Lucy not only vitiates his motive for bearing witness, but makes him sleep with her and gets convinced of his wrong reasons. Just as "trumpets preparing for another betrayal" (MW 193), he fails to protect Elizabeth from smugglers. His mind lost the last point of life in Elizabeth's stabbing, and he identifies with the man within him and takes his own life with the same knife.

An unpleasant and antagonising past and a guilt – "ridden" present blur the future. The question of "to be" or "not to be" sets in. The choice of a "not to be" should be shunned; for it neither contributes to individual's existence or society at large. Since the "already" is ailing from within, the choice of "not to be" will be destructive and detrimental. But the support of 'to be' demands an intuition that has the vitality to redress the past and build up the future. Here comes the need of a will, that does not move merely with the already known, but that can rise above the known, on its own act of volition to be on the right side of conscience which tells that good should be done and evil should be avoided. These goodness must be the motive force of our lives either in its commitments to positive ideals or in obedience to the positive promulgations of social laws or divine commandments. The circumstances that favour a "not to be" should not be permitted to dictate over the capabilities of men who can be a genuine to be. *The Man Within* illustrates it thoroughly.

The perilous plight of the 'determined' person in a filthy world thus elicits sympathy and tease the peruser's to 'reflect on the world we have left to many men around us. The form of a hunt and the indirect appeal for justice make the gestalt a perfect one. Andrews' adoration of Elizabeth and the frantic claim "I killed her". (MW 220) are points where the zest of life takes a "substitute gratification" in a wayward love and guilt. Mind deprived of a fervour annihilates the person who finds guilt in his inadequacy.

Judith Hearne or *The Lonely Passion of Judith Hearne*, the first issue of Brian Moore's fictional vigour, like Greene's *The Man Within*, is about a person who cannot find a centre to hold on to. Here too there is a constant contrast drawn between the squalor of Judith's surroundings and her expectations, her delusions, her disappointments and her disillusionments. The sordid state of affairs is filtered through her consciousness.

> Her chair is like an old pensioner starting out at the street . . . "across the worn carpet" . . . she looked away" to the white marble mantelpiece, cracked down" . . . and beside the gas fire "a sagging green covered armchair waited its human burden. The carpet below the mantelpiece was worn to brown fibre threads (JH 19).

The highly suggestive and evocative metaphorical language summarily depicts the sordid and squalid atmosphere. The chair "Sat like an old prisoner" and the 'armchair waited its human burden" are among the most consummate expressions apt to bring out the morbidity of the situation. Thus *Judith Hearne* is familiarized and defamiliarised by using a recurrent device: the investing of a material object with the power to reflect and articulate at least part of the psychic condition of the central character" (BMCS 31). The imagery here gives the readers a sense of Judith's loneliness. The repression of her life is projected in the sense of her being watched by the eyes of the wardrobe as well as by the eyes of her dead aunt. From this time to the end of the novel where she becomes reconciled to the fallen world, her adventures during that day's odyssey, in the O'Neills' house, in the presbytery, and in the church, all give evidence of her unrealized thirst for a point of escape from the seediness of life. *Judith Hearne's* interactions are limited. But even in that limited relationship, no perfect human being could be met with. Like Andrew she too is deprived of a balanced tradition. The friends too pamper her only to be victimized.

The texture of life that Brian Moore presents is subjected to such forces that make the protagonist a victim of repression, primarily religious, but also societal. The legacy to which she becomes prey is owing to Aunt d'Arcy. A religion that can serve as "a social outlet" is denied to Judith by her Aunt d'Arcy's interdiction. In the religious attitude projected when Judith and Madden go to Mass together, Judith betrays this:

> Church affairs, her aunt once said, tend to put one in contact with all sorts of people whom one would prefer not to know socially. . . . Religion was there. It was not something you thought about, and if occasionally, you had a small doubt about something in the way church affairs were carried on, or something that seemed wrong or silly, well that was the Devil at work and God's way's were not our ways. (JH 58-59)

Aunt d'Arcy's advice is an excuse to distance herself from the core of the Church. "This exclusiveness is a negation of everything that is valued by Christianity, and, furthermore, these snobbish values have done nothing but disservice to Judith in her normal social intercourse". (BMCS 18). Thus, Judith who is deprived of a religious flavour of life from the cradle, is also unlucky to meet a lover who is religious enough to inculcate a transcendental bent to her soul. For James Madden thinks:

> This was religion. Religion was begging God's pardon on a morning like this one. . . . Religion was insurance, it meant you got security afterwards. It meant you could always turn over a new leaf. . . . Mr. Madden rarely thought of purgatory, of penance. Confession and resultant absolution were the pillars of his faith. He found it comforting to start out as often as possible with a clean slate a new and promising future (JH 58).

The levity with which Madden treats religious matters add to the desacralised religious legacy of Judith, leaving her mind without an outlet, appoint of reference to tackle the crisis of life. What should be an in exhaustive reservoir of the zest of life has no mooring in her life. It gets further blurred and tarnished in the pretenses of devotion that the altar boys and priests practice.

The "bitter Comic" sermons do not serve the life of the soul. Father preaches:

> They've got time for sin, time for naked dancing girls in the cinema . . . time to dance the tango and the foxtrot and the jitter bugging, time to read trashy books and indecent magazines, time to do any blessed thing you could care to mention. Except one. They-don't-have-time-for-God (JH 64)

In the confessional box she realises that the priest is not interested in her individual life. "But she stopped speaking. She had seen his face . . . He's not listening, her mind cried, not listening" (JH 172).

Before her breakdown, she had been advised to have confession and no human sympathy was resorted to. No spirituality, no humanity to operate as a shock absorber to the ailing soul and to pour motivating and activating courage to go on is seen in her religious world.

The Catholic milieu prepared by those clergy too is "defensive" and "sectarian" rather than intimate and sympathetic. At the breakfast table in Mrs. Rice's house Lenehan accuses Madden of being an "Orangeman" rather than an Irishman. For Mr. Lenehan "most of the Catholics in this town are bloody little west Britons" (JH 81) and for Miss. Friel most of the publicans here are Catholics, it makes me see red (JH 81). After Judith's lapse into drunkenness she has to undergo alone, lonely, her earthly "passion". Charity and compassion are not at all there in the companions mind. Mr Lenehan is hypocritical in sympathy, rejoicing the 'castle' Catholic be crumbled to low. The entire situation is rightly concluded upon by John Wilson Foster as "a compassionless church and a compassionless society" (BMCS 26). In John Cronin's words: "Dismissive bitterness. . . ." (BMCS 26) is Brian Moore's consistent attitude to Belfast *Judith Hearne* is a bleak and powerful depiction of a lonely middle-class Catholic. . . . Everywhere in this powerful book there is loneliness and despair" (BMCS 26). The harsh realism is so directed to expose the hopelessness of Judith's plight that we are led to doubt with Terry Eagleton that is it not "part of the philosophical assumption of naturalism, that men are passively bound to their situations by only partially controllable forces" (BMCS 45).

In the clutches of this "seedy realm of routine social existence", her mental aberration confronts with a reality of life that does not suit to its smooth running. Failing to attain a conformity of mind with the situation outside, Judith is drowned in the deep water of guilt. A cold, alien environment, devoid of beauty and affection is her fate. Without a zest in life Judith loses her faith and she sinks in to the mire of despair, alcoholism and breakdown. Catholicism, and the society in prepares, become incapable of providing the positive force of life. According to Jo Donoghue:

> . . . religion (Catholicism) according to Moore, has no virtue as a system of ordering belief or mediating belief to the ordinary person. It is indeed, a negative force in as much as it has reference to belief: It prevents its adherents from believing in anything else, while denying them, simultaneously the joy and the fulfilment that should come with belief (BMCS 45).

Soliloquy, free indirect speech and the final third person witnesses like that of Moira O'Neill, the taxi driver and Father Quigley testify to the maladjusted personality of Judith. The familiarity of the protagonist is used to bring discernment to the reader by her harangued behaviour contrasted with James Madden, and O'Neills. The priestly figures bring in the hollowness of a superstructure compelling us to look for a point of life's flavour outside a system—in a genuine spiritual life.

The texture of life in Greene's It's a Battle Field is akin to that of *Judith Hearne*. The social background around which the action takes place is replete with mechanical and artificial relations. In the match-box factory where Kay Rimmer works, life has been reduced to a few mechanical motion: "A hand to the left, a hand to the right, the pressure of a foot . . . A hand to the left, a hand to the right, a pressure of a foot" (IBF 28). "between the cogwheels and the shafting the girls stood, as the hands of the clock moved round from eight in the morning until the (milk and biscuit at eleven) and the long drag to six" (IBF 29). Conder's field of work—the news paper office—too is not saved from this monotonous routine. In the deafening din of the typewriters that "rattled like Cavalry" (IBF 25) every one goes to this daily toil. Brian Moore's rootless ethnic society that estranges a person into loneliness and deprives him of his wholesome interaction is supplemented by Graham Greene in his It's a Battlefield. All the major characters are marooned in a contemporary waste-land a world of spiritual exptiness and material decay. It is a world of sordid commerce and glamorous slogans. In this world common cause and private agonies human hearts are torn between love and . . ., loyalty and betrayal.

The Assistant Commissioner is obsessed with Justice, whereas Conder the journalist is "a married man with a collection of foreign coins", (IBF 26) lonely and dissatisfied with his pay, profession and life. He feels that he is condemned to record the trivialities in the hope of "posthumous immortality" . . . Mr. Surrogate the fake communist is serving an unrealistic ideology, for his grand causes like social betterment, the equality of opportunity, are mere shams. He serves the cause of 'women by sleeping with them. Drover's sister-in-law Key's emancipation is from Mr. Surrogate. Kate's lover Jules Briton finds in the jolly ride and in falling in love "a very lonely stale satisfaction" (IBF 155). This is the stale, stained, and strained interactions of the modern world. "The strong disease of modern world" (IBF 39) depicted by Graham Greene.

Conrad who is aware of the hatred behind him in the school and in the office earnestly desires for justice. But he discovers that "there was no such thing as justice in the air we breathed, for it was those who hated, and envied and married for money or convenience who are happy" (IBF 62) Even his sexual intimacy with Milly is an act of hate: Holding her body close to him with painful tenderness, it was hate he chiefly felt, hate of Jim, of two men laughing in Piccadilly. The shape of a society sifted out of such rootless interaction is brought out in Conrads failure and death. It is the last word against a society:

> that condemns men in to shells of loneliness and then make the rules to govern its prisoners . . .. . others had made the rules by which he suffered; it was unfair that they should leave him so a one and yet make the rules which governed him (IBF 159).

In Brian Moore the tabernacle remains silent and in Greenes novels the promulgations of Social laws take their silent course on people whom the society itself make a victim.

The contrast in the attitude to life and the need of an ennobling point of configuration are pointed out in the persons of the commissioner and caroline Bury. For the former life "is a great waste, a useless expenditure of lives" and he does not find "a great directing purpose in the world." (IBF 191). His praise for Bury's faith is really a lauding of the search for the point of zest in life.

Whatever she means by it" (IBF, 192) he takes Bury's faith to justify his superstition" "one had to choose certain superstition by which to live; they were the nails in the shoes with which one gripped the rock" (IBF 170) The Assistant Commissioner in genuine mental agony bewails: "If I had faith, he though wryly, if I had any conviction that it was on the right side' Caroline has that, when she chooses it, she has only to change her side (IBF 201-202). This is the poignant agony of a man without a zest of conviction to go on in life.

A drab world, and without the nexus of love in interaction where everybody is "too busy fighting his own little battle to think of . . . the next man" (IBF 188) where can we find a root to zest in life? In Justice? In Respect? In love? In ethics? John Atkins agrees with us when he writes:

> There is not an ounce of encouragement. Not even the catholic faith is trotted out with its consolations. The characters either admit vacancy or fall back on pretenses.[2]

Above the absurdity of life, can we posit an value system a myth, a being? for an urge to go on, a point to hand on?

Jim Drover's imprisonment for killing a policeman at a Communist meeting and the ensuing attempt to reprieve after the failure of an appeal are depicted as the Zenith of the shams and hollowness of interactions. The interaction of his wife, brother, sister-in-law, the police commissioner, and the Assistant Secretary momentously moves for the reprieve. But in this battle none of them is sure of their motives. And each one is left to serve each ones' end. Milly's love loses its virility in thinking of a long lapse of eighteen years of prison life and Conrad too is enmeshed in the same cobweb snare of thinking ending in 'shameful remorse' of fornication. Conrad then loses his motive though he runs after the police commissioner and gets knocked down. Does Milly and Jim have one? not at all.

Thus in *It's a Battlefield*, a world of material decay, filth, failure betrayal and spiritual emptiness are depicted in a very realistic life situation. It takes us to the picture of world given by Matthew Arnold in "Dover Beach":

> The world, which seems to lie before us
>
> Like a land of dreams so various, so beautiful, so new,
>
> Hath really neither joy, nor love, nor light
>
> Nor certitude, nor peace, nor help for pain;

And we are here as on a darkling plain

Sweft with confused alarms of struggle and flight

Where ignorant armies clash by night.[3]

This ignorant bliss in which the armies fight is brought to us through the epigraph from Kinglake:

> Insofar as the battlefield presented itself to the bare eyesight of men, it had no entirety, no length, no breadth, no depth, no size, no shape . . . in such conditions each separate gathering of English soldiery went on fighting its own little battle in happy and advantageous ignorance of the general state of the action, may even very often in ignorance of the fact that any great conflict was ranging (IBF 2).

Brian Moore sketches the same battle-field in *The Emperor of Ice-Cream* (1965). Gavin Burke in his young age is forced to be limited by alien forces and is trapped in powerlessness. All his reforming zeal and vision rooted in W.B. Yeasts, Louis Mac Neice's, Clifford Odetes and Wallace Steven's Philosophy, get choked up by the intervention of adult world. He is motivated to rebel against the sexual, religious and intellectual imposition. And Sally Shannon despite her allurement is another domestic strain. He eventually realizes that the only true emperor is the *Emperor of Ice-Cream*.

> His life since leaving school had been a see-saw going up to the height of the grown up world. . . . In both worlds, lack of purpose, lack of faith, was the only deadly sin. In both worlds the authorities, detecting that sin arranged one's punishment. All of life's races are fixed and false you stand at the starting line, knowing you can run as well as the others, but the authorities, those inimical and unknown arbiters, have decreed that you will not get off your marks. They know . . . that your future will be void. (EIC 191-92).

What flavour of life is left in this great realisation after the service in F.A.P and A.R.P.? The cold, legalistic, pedantic and unimaginative father, standing in his own condemned house is no more an authoritarian will. But "His father was a child now, his fathers world was dead" (ELC 250). His father is man of this change. Oh Gavin, his father said: I have been a fool. Such a fool The Black Angel and 'White Angel' gives place to a new voice. The new voice counseled silence. He looks at fathers hand. "Nothing but a silence is left to follow for the old world is dead" (EIC 251).

The society that Graham Greene depicts in *England Made Me* is similar to that of the society depicted by Brian Moore in *Emperor of Ice-Cream*. Greene's milieu of *It's a Battlefield* further enhances the pattern and life mentioned in former novels. The loss of a deep interaction based on values and love; the estrangement of the past and the present run in all these fictions. Cosmopolitan Stockholm and suburban London are the two worlds that clash for predominance in *It's a Battlefield*. This shakes Kate out of her false identification causing her to leap for a divine moment. But majority of characters are caught in the tragic trap of here and now and doom themselves to a meaningless life. The themes of isolation and betrayal fill the novel with the atmosphere of failure and frustration. Erik Krogh represents the industrial and material success over the nationalistic values of England. He is the centre around which, like spokes of a wheel turns certain English characters, like Anthony, Rate Farrant, and Minty. As the industrial horizon expands, values in the interrelationships of these people are distorted and human and divine values too are erased out of each one's life contributing to their disfigured personalities.

Erik Krogh is a business tycoon. He rules over his business empire: "Krogh like God almighty in every home" (EMM 21). He lives for amassing wealth. His success at last serves only to degrade his humanity. He is fortified by his mind-made citadel: "E.K. on the ashtray; E.K. on the carpet; E.K. flashing above the fountain which he watched, above the gateway; he was surrounded by himself (EMM 49). He doesn't know jokes and laughs and his relationship with Kay, his mistress and secretary is futile; for human beings are not his domain: "He was quite happy again, because he was dealing with figures . . . there was nothing human about them" (EMM 131). This centre will not hold, no, it doesn't hold. For poetry, art and music are things he doesn't understand, and human qualities like decency and honesty are alien to him: "Honesty was a word which had never troubled him: a man was honest so long as his credit was good: and his credit, he could tell himself with pride, stood a point higher than the credit of the French Government (EMM 35). When he suspects anything harmful to this sky-high credit, he practices fraud. Thus Anderson, his son and Anthony, fall prey to his cunning selfishness.

Hall loses all his personality, in upholding the values of Krogh. Materialism manifests its ferocious and when Krogh uses Hall to eliminate his foes.

Minty the journalist who makes his living by reporting on Krogh "had been slowly broken in by parents, by school masters and strangers in the Street" (EMM 72). And now he is moved only by the "squalid necessity of earning money (EMM 71). His claim that "I'm a religious man" (EMM 76) should be assessed from his reaction to human presence: "Yes it was ugly, the human figure, Man or Women it made no difference to Minty" (EMM 87). He shuns wine and has a distrust of women. Thus minty searches for a point of zest in life, that does not materialise in reality. Even the religion he practices is crude.

Anthony Farrant, Kates brother is full-fledged in failure. He remarks about himself 'that he was dusty'. "The grit of London lay under his eyes, he was at home in the swirl of smoke and steam . . ."(EMM 12) persuasion of Kate on him succeeds and he too is succumbed to the power of money. But the valueless reality behind the "glassy clearness" of this world shocks him and he is" too innocent to live." (EMM 186).

In Anthony's failure to fit in to Krogh's world of progress brings out the contrast in the relationship between Anthony and Kate Farrant, though they shares the same past. Their relationship recedes in the lack of communication. They experience the curse of ceasing to know each other. "According to Loo, their relationship in so limiting (EMM 129) she puzzles him with the humanity of success, but in his conceited failure he admits: "I haven't a future, Kate" (EMM 29) Graham Greene differentiates the 'here' in which Anthony belongs and the 'there' Kate cherishes: "Here was the twin dials on the gas-motor meter, the dirty pane .. . the familiar photographs, the pawned bags, the empty pockets, home" (EMM 15).

And 'there' was

> ... the glassy cleanliness, the latest fashionable sculpture, the sound proof floors .. . and Erik in his silent rooms listening to reports from Warsaw, Amster dam, Paris and Berlin (EMM 15)

This contrast of the values of Anthony and Kate, is a clash of the values of suburban London and cosmopolitan Stockholm. Kate later gets bewilders of her identification. She feels the loss of identity and even prayer gives place to plan. She remains sterile in all her plans; for Anthony's death put an end to her clinging habit and she realises that:

> He are'll thieves' stealing a livelihood here and there and everywhere, giving nothing back . .. No brotherhood in our boat. Only who can cut the biggest dash and who can swim." (EMM 206)

This is the lost patch of ground that we experience in modern industrialise London-City. And we too with Kate, Say I am not going to this city any more; but "No, I am simply moving on, Like Anthony (EMM 207) Anthony stands for those men who fail miserably in life due to lack of adequate point of the flavour of life in the material progress of our growth.

Here is the world where the best lack all conviction and simply move in life, in the company of seediness, solitariness, and selfishness, lost in the madding crowd.

This overriding secular tenor that permeates the interactions of men is vehemently complemented by Brian Moore, in *The Temptation of Eileen Hughes* and *The Colour of Blood* Greene suggestively and satirically evinces how materialism can be a threat to the flavour of life whereas Brian Moore takes the sublimative instinct of the impotent ex-priest Bernard MacAuley who equates his sex drive with religious zeal and exposes the possibility of an "ego-mania", when man is deprived of right religious spirit. Mona has not yet borne for him a child and his aesthetic sensibility that could not be materialised in former vocation looks for a substitute. In a quasi-religious terms, Bernard says: "But having you here so close, having you all to myself in London, seeing Kenwood, having you say, that you wanted to live in a big house, it was too great a temptation (TEH 77).

The Temptation he feels is so strong that he tries to save himself in an identity with his idol:

> I am trying to save myself, not save the world. I told you, when I was twenty I wanted to be a saint, to save my soul, to love God, to do good. But it seems I won't wanted in that way . . . until I met you, until that day I saw you standing in the shop, I never knew what real happiness was (TEH 76).

Modern psychology agrees that it has nothing to do with religious experience but is mere ego-mania. Carl Jung described religion as:

> A careful and scrupulous observation of the 'Numinosum' that is, a dynamic agency or effect not caused by an arbitrary act of the will. . . . The

> numinosum-whatever its cause may be- is an experience of the subject independent of his will. . . . The Numinosum is either a quality belonging to a visible object or the influence of an invisible presence that causes a peculiar alteration of consciousness.[4]

To Jung the world religion means a careful consideration and observation of certain dynamic factors that are conceived as 'power', 'spirits'. . . . Laws, ideals or . . . to such factors in his world as he has found powerful, dangerous or helpful enough to be taken in to careful consideration or grand, beautiful, and meaningful enough to be devoutly worshipped and loved.[5] But Bernard McAuley's numinosum is a person, not a power, or a spirit or an ideal. His obsession ends in religious sickness – a mania. "To serve a mania is detestable and undignified, but to serve a god is full of meaning and promise because it is an act of submission to a higher, invisible and spiritual being".[6] Thus, the "substitute gratification" that can serve as a flavour of life for a short span, has proved destructive. The suicide of Bernard McAuley in *The Temptation of Eileen Hughes'* verifies the fact and argues for an unchanging power as the cause, reason and finality of life's zest.

This apparently obsessive striving for substitute gratification has taken sociological dimension in *The Colour of Blood* where Cardinal Bem, though a dedicated divine has canalized his zest. Brian Moore confesses that the country in question in this novel is fictional.

> I specifically synthesized a country of my mind, an Eastern European country that could be Hungary, or Czechoslovakia or Ireland . . . When I say Ireland, I am perfectly serious. I took my descriptions of searches and check points from my experience in Ireland rather than Eastern Europe. That is I wasn't trying to make any comparison between the occupation of Northern Ireland and the Russian presence in Poland. But at the back of my mind there are connections. If we cannot

live with each other and run our own affairs someone will be brought in to run things for us" (BMCS 219).

Thus, it appears that politics takes on the colour of morality in the author at this stage.

The final challenge that the author poses to reason is another internal evidence that substantiates the argument.

The Cardinal reads from St. Bernard of Clairvaux:

> Do you think that a man born with reason yet not living according to this reason is, in a certain way, no better than the beast themselves? For the beast who doesn't rule himself by reason has an excuse, since this gift is denied him by nature. But man has no excuse (CB 2).

In the entire novel reason is contrasted with the unreasoning fanaticism of the assassin. The world of his duties is a world of unreason for Bem. To strike at the penury of reason is a great realisation, that the purest spirituality can be sought in closer communion with God in contemplation of life. In this bent of mind Cardinal Bem seeks a via-media of political pragmatism. But Archbishop Krasnky is all for an imminent revolution. His inflammatory metaphorical speech reads:

> The nation in this critical time is like a great forest at the end of a summer of dreadful drought, a spiritual and moral drought. On the floor of this forest are millions of pine needles. It takes only a spark to set them ablaze (CB 13).

The novel turns to a definite secular cause - politics - as a zest for action in Cardinal Bem, when he realises the insidious movements of one group of clergy and the terrorists. The incinerating political climate is clear when politics and religious are mixed or confused:

> I think our people are using religion now as a sort of politics. To remind ourselves that we are a catholic nation while our enemies are not, to remind us that we always continued to be a nation even when the name of our country was take off the map, It's all part of our collective memory and we cherish it. But what has it got to do with our love of God? (CB 116)

Impelled by the love of God he resolves to stop the seditious speech of the Bishop on Martyr's day. He is totally taken up by the political turmoil in the Bishop's conference and he prays:

> I am your servant, seated by you. All that I have through you and from you. Nothing is my own. I must do everything for you and only for you. Tonight at the meeting I was obsessed by politics; I thought of the danger of our nation. I did not think of the sufferings we cause you by our actions. My fault, my own grievous fault. (CB 18).

Though he survives the house arrest and moral inoculations, his zeal for the nation cannot surmount the bullet while giving away the holy Eucharist. Brian Moore depicts the plenitude in the fervour of life for a secular cause by a divine. Brian Moore places the Cardinal against his own split factions of Bishops and the terrorists and in the midst of the faithful. When he undergoes the hardships of a journey and preaches on the martyr's day, our thrill gets converted to anxious curiosity. When the Martyr's day creates another martyr, we recall the first attempt on his life, his house arrest, the stealthy journey and the cunning craftiness with which he manages the hostile scenario. Finally we are led to a question: Does political stability deserve this much sacrifice and dedication?

In *The Colour of Blood,* Brian Moore searches for political stability and peaceful co-existence of religion, where as in Graham Greene's *The Power and the Glory,* the entire devouring attitude of politics and its 'force of habit' on people thoroughly annihilates the Whisky priest. The priest falls on the physical and moral plane, yet converts even the Marxist lieutenant - when he calls a priest for the confession of his victim - zest takes its religious dimension like that of the spring of action of Father Lafargue in Brian Moore's Black Robe.

Graham Greene wrote in *The Lawless Road*

> People must have something outside the narrow world to life for - whether it is the idea of the inevitable progress of the proletarian revolution or just that a black cat will bring them luck if it crosses their path (TLR 83).

With this metaphysical urge for life he visited Mexico and found that "life was happier with enormous supernatural promise than with the petty social furniture' (TLF 83). Africa with its devil dance and aboriginal cruelties and dances represented to Greene 'a strangeness, a wanting to know." Graham Greene's African journey represented "a distrust of any future based on what we are". He was torn between two beliefs: "The belief that life should be better than it is and the belief that when it appears better it really worse" (JWM 82). This disputed territory of Graham Greene's belief gets a transcendental unity in *The Power and the Glory* where the priest, falls in his physical and moral life but not in the purpose of the vocation. Here faith is the sole impelling factor of action. The whisky priest bears the burnt of the whole normlessness of the physical, social and political world. This is the culmination of Graham Greene's search for a source of zest in life. *The Man Within*, *England Made Me*, *It's a Battlefield*, *A Gun For Sale* are mere backgrounds illustrating the aspects of deprivation of mankind. He discovers that there is moral, aesthetic and intellectual perversions in humanity and its fundamental defect lies in the family and the social milieu. Therefore a search for unity of human action in faith is the last word that Graham Greene utters in *The Power and the Glory*.

Just as Graham Greene has a liberating conception of political activity, Brian Moore too believes in a political purpose in his early writing.

> I do believe that for a novelist to have something to react against, to have something to fight against, to be dissatisfied, to be an outsider, to be a person who has some almost moralistic mission, to correct what he considers to be an injustice or a wrong way of living, is probably his strength, will start him writing and may even keep him writing (BMCS 219).

It is this fire of conviction that is brought out in *Lies of Silence through Dillon*.

> And now . . . Dillon felt anger rise within him, anger at lies which made this ... lies told over the years to poor protestant working people about the catholic, lies told to poor Catholic working people about the Protestants . .. the lies of silence from those in Westminster who did not want to face the injustice of ulster's *status quo* (LS 49).

The explication of faith in action reaches it's zenith in Brian Moore in *Catholics*, *Black Robe*, and *The Colour of Blood.* In *Catholics*, Fr. James Kinsella and Abbot Thomas Malley present faith in its secular phase with the internal tension culminating ultimately in the surrender of the will. Basically there is not much difference in the spirit of *The Power and the Glory* and the *Catholics*. In *The Power and the Glory* and whisky priest is pitted against a communist lieutenant and the fight of the two wills—the secular and the religious—reaches its finale in the physical and spiritual surrender of the priest when he is shot down proclaiming, 'Jai Christ the King'. When the abbot kneels down in the chapel (after quietening the rebellion of his co-priests and monks in the monastery), praying 'our father in heaven . . .

he too verifies the power and the glory of God. Thus, the terror terrane of *The Power and the Glory* ends in surrender of life; the tension terrane of *Catholics* ends in the surrender of the will.

What is left as an open gestalt by Greene in, *The Man Within, England Made Me* and *It's a Battle Field* in the lack of faith and spirituality, is answered in *The Power and the Glory*, what is left as an open gestalt in *Judith Hearne, An Answer from Limbo, I am Mary Dunne, The Feast of Lupercal, The Great Victorian Collection, The Temptation of Eileen Hughes* and *Cold Heaven*, is explicated in *Black Robe*, the *Catholics* and *The Colour of Blood*. *In the former Belfast novels*, the impediments in the growth of the catholic personality is brought out, whereas in the latter novels, a clear answer is rendered in depicting faith as the zest of life. Brian Moore remarks: "I have always been interested in the fact that people must believe in something—nuclear disarmament, love as a generating force, politics or anything"[7], Later he says:

> I found, when I started to write, and became very interested in the question of faith . . . the virtue of having a belief in something. I began to see and to feel, as I do now, that the great lack of modern life is the lack of belief in something greater than ourselves (BMCS 15).

Moore admits this similarly of a governing passion in Greene. "I think it was Greene who said that the governing passion lends unity to any shelf of books" (BMCS 11). Elizabeth Bowen assents "A man's whole art may be rendered down, by analysis, to variations upon a single theme" (BMCS 11).

Man's search for the sap of life in the absurd contexts of life often takes on the colour of a religious search. But Greene and Moore contrast individuals against society and change the pattern. Norman Sherry, for example, illustrates this turn when he remarks that "the religious theme changes (Brighton Rock) from a story about gang warfare into a struggle between Good and Evil set against a representative background of human society."[8] A.A. Devitis, commenting on the allegory in *Brighton Rock*, too arrives at the same conclusion:

> Moving from the world of *Stamboul Train* (1932) and *A Gun for Sale* into that of *Brighton Rock* is much like moving from the square of a medieval village into the dim-light of the cathedral to contemplate God under the storied capital where the demons and angels battle for the Soul of a Man.[9]

This description of life as an arena where a man has to take care of his soul is a positive stroke in the march of man towards that eternal beach.

This search for the spiritual spring of man, in Graham Greene, says Jeffery Mayers, perhaps owing to the influence of T.S. Eliot's famous essay on Baudelaire. This applies to Greene's *Catholic* characters like Pinkie. About Baudelaire Eliot has written:

> He was one of those who had great strength, but strength merely to suffer. He could not escape suffering and could not transcend it. So he attracted pain to himself. But what he could do with that immense passover strength and sensibilities which no pain could impair, was to study his suffering. . . . In his way suffering is already a kind of presence of the supernatural and of the superman. . . . His ennui is a true form of 'acedia' arising from the unsuccessful struggle towards the spiritual life.[10]

Throughout Greene's work there is an attempt to synchronise the spiritual and earthly realm of existence. Thus the squalor and filth, the wearying and warring forces are provided to show the relation between incommensurable and hostile forces, between incompatible worlds, between the moral world of right and wrong and to represent the dynamism of life.

This theme of the basic confrontation of the two levels of existence, the spiritual and the earthly, seems to have a close affinity with the theme of different levels of conscience in existentialist philosophy. An individual's awareness of the moral code accepted by the society and the individuals conviction that transcends the accepted standards of society are the two kinds of conscience. The existentialist values man's deeper level of conscience—the one which can transcend conventional morality. No one can escape the clash between these two levels of conscience. Kierkegaard in his *Fear and Trembling* in the story of Abraham and Isaac elucidates this clash. Abraham is ready to go against moral principles and human feelings to obey God's command. The universal, natural order or the public conscience is laid aside in his duty towards God. This dynamism of the spirit is graphically presented in Graham Greene's *Catholic Trilogy* and the novels of the initial phase illustrate the clash of conscience.

In this dynamism of the spirit either in the form of contrasted conscience or the basic confrontation of the spiritual and the mundane, the zest for life is sought by Graham Greene as well as Brian Moore. In the insipidity of life Brian Moore unearths "a Great Absence" and argues for "a Great presence". Jenny Flood assesses the Central Situation in the novels of Brian Moore as that of the deep sense of a great absence. Judith terribly longs for a great presence in the tabernacle, but it remains tacit. Since the social harmony too is broken in the loss of a great brotherhood, that could compensate this urge, she undergoes a breakdown. But in the later novels including the recent one, Bernard MacAuley, Anthony, Davine Darmund, Gavin Burke and Dhillon desperately search for this presence in mere secular fetish objects, and taste failure.

But the mind of the divines in Greene's and Brian Moores' novels find their source of action in the words of Jesus:

"whoever is thirsty let him come to me and drink: he who believes in me just as the scripture says, streams of water will flow from his innermost being." (John 7: 37, 38). The source of their fervour is the grace of God that they feel in the very core of their life. This divine love enables them to forget themselves and to interrelate audaciously with secular, spiritual or to undertake any hazardous missionary endeavours. There is no division of secular or religious when these divines are transformed in the smithy of faith. This internal enlightenment that enables them to be in the hand of universal charity grants them meaning and significance in life.

Thus the pattern and life that both the novelists expose in their divergent technique indicate to the need of a point of drive, a flavour of life that gets its impetus from within and will solve the dichotomy of within and without by cementing matured right relationship to make this journey of life a beautiful one.

NOTES

1. W.B. Yeast, 'The Second Coming', *Twentieth Century Verse* ed. C.T. Thomas (Madras: Macmillan, 1979) 62.
2. John Atkins, *Graham Greene*, (London: John Calder, 1957) 38.
3. C.B. Tinker and H.F. Lowry, *The Poetry of Matthew Arnold* (London: Oxford UP, 1940) 175.
4. Carl Gustav Jung, *Jung: Selected Writings*, (London: Fontana, 1983) 239-40.
5. *Ibid*, 239-40.
6. *Ibid*, 239-40.
7. Joyce Andrews, 'Education through the Writer's Eye', diss, (Dublin: University of Dublin, 1984) 157.
8. Norman Sherry, *The Life of Graham Greene*, Vol.1 (London: Jonathan Cape, 1989) 636.
9. A.A. Devitis, *Graham Greene* (New York: Twayne Publishers, 1964) 66.
10. Jeffrey Meyers, ed, *Graham Greene. A Revaluation* (Hamshire: Macmillan, 1990) 140.

6 CONCLUSION

Although both are Catholics, Graham Greene and Brian Moore differ in their Christian background. The former was a converted Catholic, who shared Protestant faith and Marxist ideology in his early life, whereas Brian Moore was born and brought up by Catholic parents. He was nourished an nurtured in Catholic schools and colleges. As an insider he felt the stifling weight of a dogmatic system. Thus, the outsider's search for an infallible value system and an insider's clamour for individuality in Catholic life converge in Graham Greene and Brian Moore. From a thematic point of view, both the writers reiterate the need of a cause to live for. The crisis through which both the writers allow their protagonists to pass through, and the ethos from which these men try to flee in search of a new value system point to the inadequacy of the existing social milieu and its values. Both of them concentrate on losers because, as Brian Moore feels, failure is a more interesting condition than success. Success changes people; it makes them something they are not and dehumanises them in a way that leaves you with a more intense distillation of the self you are.

The Catholic community is counted as the embodiment of the logos of God. Therefore, it is regarded by both novelists as the living cenotaph, the "mustard seed" that shelters the birds and the "yeast"[1] that forms as the catalyst in the transformation of the world. Thus, the "isomorphic unit of experience"[2] that Gestalt critics try to find in any artistic work is sought here in the theological background of the Catholic Church. For "the internal perceptual field"[3] that the protagonists nurture and the "fictional finalism"[4] they develop in their confrontation of reality as "life-force" get their backward and forward movement for an efficient as well as final cause in the divine presence of the Church. The ego and the indoctrinised ego get sifted through in the intervention of the divine light. The theological transcendence sought here follows the reflection of Maximus, the confessor—the towering figure of Byznatine tradition and also Vladimir Solovyev, the central figure of Russian spirituality. Their reflections based on the Gospel of St. John 1:1 is highly relevant in explicating the title of this book. According to Maximum in God the ideas (logoi) of all things are fixed; thus it is said that God knows all things before they come forth; for they are in him and with him as he is the very truth of all that exists, even things in their totality. That is to say, those that are and those that are yet to be, do not come into existence simultaneously; but each one comes into existence at the time predetermined for it. "All things created are defined, both in their being and in their becoming, by their own particular ideas or logoi and by the ideas of other existents which are externally proximate to them and the existence are thus circumscribed by their ideas."[5]

But this multiplicity of logoi is constituted by a single logos which is their unifying principle. The logos in its unity is transcendent, while in it's multiplicity it remains immanent in particular existents. Humanity thus becomes predetermined by the idea of man. Here freedom plays a lesser role. The necessity to define humanity by its original model, namely, the divine logos himself who became the Son of man, and the conformity to this incarnated logos, are demanded from us for us to be perfect.

Therefore, to be a genuine human being is to be related to the whole humanity is indispensable. Each created existence is, not simply "to be", but "to be in a particular way." A created being 'is' only in a particularly qualified way, in a particular relationship to others. This essential, existential communion with other existents is the other transcendence which is pointed out in the gestalt of experience in the fictions of Graham Greene and Brian Moore. Temporality and finitude must go together, and when man experiences full salvation, he will move out of temporality into eternity, which is the proper mode of existence of God himself. The life of the human being is a progressive movement, from birth to the fullness of being. Therefore, the trilogic aspects of human ego "to be", "to be good" and "to be forever" (genesis-kinesis-stasis) are the phases of personality too. "To be" and "to be for ever" are the gifts of God, but "to be good" is a contribution of our own free will. Until we reach eternity, which is the boundary of this becoming, the urge to be good "leads" us through successive stages of alienation, nausea, world-weariness and desperate predicaments. This cosmic search of man tied up in a microcosm that claims to be an ideal one, take a suppressing factor of humanity. The threatening dimensions of a dogmatic system thus appears to be against the fullness of humanity. This constitutes the weariness of the protagonists of the Belfast novels of Brian Moore.

According to Solovyev, Wisdom or Sophia existed before the creation of the world, eternally in the bosom of the Father, along with the logos. The logos is the producing principle; Sophia is the actualizing one.

Applying the principle that 'the whole is prior to its parts and is presupposed by them', Solovyev insists that the whole humanity is prior to individual human beings, and thus constitutes one organic whole. He then concludes that Sophia is no other than the true, pure and perfect humanity, the highest and all-embracing form and the living soul of nature and universe united to God from all eternity and in the temporal process attaining union with him and uniting to him all that is."[6] It is meant in the first instance, that we should treat our social and cosmic environment as an actual living being with which we are in the closest and most complete interaction, without ever being merged in it. In order that the false separation of beings in space and time should be abolished altogether, and all individuals, both past and present should become eternal, the process of integration must transcend the limits of social or strictly human life and include the cosmic sphere from which it started. In ordering the physical world, the divine idea had thrown the veil of natural beauty over the kingdom of matter and death; through man, through the activity of his universally rational consciousness, it must then enter the kingdom from within in order to give life to nature and make its beauty eternal. In this sense it is essential to change man's relation to nature. He must enter with the same relation of Syzygic unity which determines his true life in the personal and social sphere.

Every conscious human activity, determined by the idea of universal Syzygy and having its purpose the embodiment of the all embracing ideal in some particular here, actually produces or liberates spiritually - material currents which gradually gain possession of the material environment, spiritualize it and embody in it certain images of the all-embracing unity. The spiritual energy is trapped in the protagonists of Graham Greene and Brian Moore, so that the heroes cannot take the role of a life force to create a love relationship to create spiritual energies which inwardly transform the Cosmos, imprinting upon it the image of God as love. The cosmos itself is a living organism within which the "pleroma" of humanity as an organ has a central and key function almost like the heart or brain in the body. Sophia is both humanity and the earth principle, the Magna Mater. The construction of humanity itself is a mediating principle between God and nature.

Just as the logic of the *Bible* is a search from disorder to order Graham Greene and Brian Moore seek that hovering spirit in the chaos of modern man. Politics, cybernetics, religion, psychology and science are all employed by both the novelists to explore the turmoils and muddled state of affairs and to contribute to the need of "a great presence".

In *I am Mary Dunne* if the heroine shares the same neurotic plight of *Freud's Dora*, in *The Man Within, Brighton Rock* and *The Heart of the Matter*, individual psyche in its childhood as well as adolescent phases are explicated to bring out the tension of the "already" and "not yet" of human psyche.

The violent and political setting through which the novelists take us in *The Power and the Glory, Monsignor Quixote, Black Robe* and *The Colour of Blood* are for dramatizing the withering away of the private and the public worlds. The paternity that the heroes search for in these novels are the spiritual rationality or the same cerebral life to which the initial novels of both Graham Greene and Brian Moore point to. In "the clash of the ignorant armies" we are challenged to a commitment, in the loss of the glory of humanity we are grieved, inducing us to participate in the whole for what the part lacks.

Graham Greene explores a fallen world for the "appalling strangeness of God's mercy" to operate in the new predicament of men. In Brian Moore's Belfast novels he does not allow them to be entangled by ritualistic routine and an imposing community and paternity. This search for freedom ends in a realisation of the need of a cosmic humanity and prepares the way for the mercy of God to operate.

These angry men who have their moorings in the Catholic Church depict violence to project the inner disharmony of modern man due to the present encompassings and also as guardian angels they indicate solutions in novels like *The Human Factor, The Quiet American, The Honorary Consul* and *The Lies of Silence, Revolution Script, The Colour of Blood* and *Black Robe*. But the underlying tenet in both the novelists is the total experience of life transcending the political and social man. The violence that Fr. Laforgue confronts in Huron land and Cardinal Bem suffers in Europe and the whisky priest resists in his hide-outs is for an order. The "terrible beauty" and the "terrible aboriginal calamity" that envelop modern man are depicted by both to achieve a catharsis as well as to design a way out. At the end of each novel, both Graham Greene and Brian Moore do not leave us in escathological waiting but challenge us to audacious decisions to be a part of a salvific process.

The powerful sexual drive that Graham Greene and Brian Moore portray even in the most arduously sought out missionary enterprise has given them the nomenclature "obsessional". Brian Moore's Judith is terribly shaken by the discovery of Fadden's identity. The impotent Bernard turns to a substitute gratification in *The Temptation of Eileen Huge's* and Gavin Burke in *Emperor of Ice-cream* is disgusted in his foiled attempt to kiss Sally Shannon, finds a reconciliation with his father. Fadden's life in California is made a 'comedy segment with the Danises in Fergus. In Cold Heaven Marie Davenport Symbolises "bad faith" in modern world and Mary in *I am Mary Dunne* inherits guilt from the death-bed of her father. Anthony Maloney's artistic life is in jeopardy in his relationship with his wife, Secretary Ann, and even with his mother. Daniel deserts Laforgue for the sake of Anuka, and for culture that is untainted by a mania for possession. At the expense of his beloved, Dhillon is involved in the *IRA Bombing* in *The Lies of Silence*. Thus in Brian Moore sex and family life is seen in the isomorphic unit of experience of liberation and bondage, often bringing out as impeding the artistic and aesthetic realization as in the case of Brendan in *An Answer from Limbo*.

But to Andrews in *The Man Within and Conrad* in It's a *Battle Field* the sexual act means a betrayal; it means "the last human shame" to Pinkie in Brighton Rock. To the whisky priest sex is corruption but to Scobie it is a love that begs divine mercy. *To Bendrix in The End of the Affair*, sex means jealous, egoistic possession, but for Sarah his beloved, sex means ordinary corrupt human love that is a way for greater sanctity. But there are others too who play with sex; for Anthony Farrant (*England Made Me*) Sex is an adolescent pastime, but to Kate it is a natural drive. To Kay Rimer in It's a Battlefield sex brings "the deep peace of sensuality".

Like Brian Moore, Graham Greene too treats sexual indulgence associated with guilt and sadness. Love and lust and immoral sex foster alienation, corruption, guilt, betrayal. In other words both Graham Greene and Brian Moore suggest to remedy the sordid state of affairs in the present predicament of man through the right perception of sex life and family life. Sexual life should drive at the development of qualities of cosmic common humanity not to foster parts' self assertion, but to the emergence of the whole. You and I must form a we. What underlies their presentation is a metaphysical leap from what we are to what we ought to be.

In the search for an order of psyche in faith and genuine identity, as John Wilson Foster puts it, "the community's ritual leads to crisis" and later longs for "a great presence"[7] by the protagonists of both the novelists.

This search for the great presence among the Hurons is the theme of *Black Robe* and in the arduous process of making this presence felt, Cardinal Bem has to holocaust his life among the divided factions of Bishops and their terrorists in *The Colour of Blood*. The void of this Great presence drive men to egomania and the suicide of a business man in *The Temptations of Eileen Hughes* and that of a creative scholarly artist in *The Great Victorian Collection*. There is a desperate attempt to compensate the lost presence in a cultural heritage in *The Mangan Inheritance*. But it ends in the distorted and reaffirmed reiteration on the question of self-identity.

But the dogmatic Catholic commitment in Greene's novel though obvious in the conscious and subconscious mind of most of the heroes, cannot easily be located in a particular domain of dogmatic theology. In the interplay of loyalty and betrayal, innocence and corruption, religions faith and political commitment, the dominating pattern of doubt and questionings characters search for a belief. The Catholic characters like Pinkie, Rose, Scobie, the whisky priest and Sarah Miles have fallen prey to the temptations of flesh. Their consciousness of sin and guilt justifies the doctrine of original sin. At the same time, the seriousness with which the Christ figures are risen, and sanctity given to Sarah Miles in The End of the Affair the tragi-cosmic vision of A Burnt out Case has to be equated with Brian Moor's longing for a divine humanhood in his protagonists. The "megasynthesis" and the "christogenesis" that occur at the end of *The Power and the Glory* and Monsignor Quixote in Greene's fiction are synchronized in the miraculous mission of Father Laforgue in *Black Robe* and the blood of cardinal Bem that serves as water for the growth of Christianity in *The Colour of Blood*. With Wordsworth we too must say, dull would be the man who cannot stand and look at the these heroes and cannot develop a dedication and zeal for duty and life.

The tantalizing evasive vision that is brought out form the rough periphery of modern interaction, keeps both Graham Greene and Brian Moore gravely aware of technique while translating this vision. There is a clever use of structure and cinematic devices by Graham Greene. Ornamental expression and laboriously imaginative structured details furnish the sentiments and drabness of the muddled affairs of men. Dramatic dialogues and dreams are aptly used by both the novelists to bring out the strife of modern psyche. We may be astounded at the torturing of the protagonists by both the novelists, but it is to shake our imagination and to "shock us to freedom" and to make us discern the "freedom" in which we are steeped. Whereas the interior monologues in Graham Greene's novels make us aware of the thought processes of men and women in society, the first and third person narratives in Brian Moore bring out the disharmony and discord of the objective and subjective experience. The miracles and religiosity augment the psyche's pangs for a belief. Graham Greene's as well as Brian Moore's heroes and heroines are objective co-relatives who stand for the "isomorphic unit of experience" that render a legitimacy to imaginative life, teasing us to change from our "taught life" to "felt life" and then to a 'thought life", to make life in this" most beloved earth more lovely".

Bereft of support and lacking unity with perfect humanity, these protagonists not only alienate bur form a "fictional finalism" of their own to live on; often ending in monomaniacal tendencies and suicide. None of them says 'I am O.K. (in terms of transactional analysis) and the parent, adult and child in each of them do not find a sublimating point. So in their image making process, the art of iconopeia, they project an ideal future and try to work out a real future. This "image making calls" for a measure of direct experience of the transcendent. Without some asceticism and mystical experience, intuition and ecstacy, genuine practice of the art of iconopeia is virtually impossible. This fact is elucidated in the protagonists of both the novelists. Oliver Reiser in his *Cosmic Humanism* advances the hypothesis that "men are the embryonic cells (neuroblasts) of an emerging world organism ... we are participating in the embryogenesis of a giant organism".[8] He conceived the planet earth as a psychosomatic creature with the organized humanity forming its brain cortex. The protagonists whom we have seen are in search of that brain cortex which has not met within the given social milieu.

NOTES

1. *Holy Bible* Matthew, 13: 31-32.
2. Paul Edwards, *Gestalt Theory: The Encyclopaedia of Philosophy* Vol. 8 (New York: Collier Macmillan, 1972) 318.

3. Alfred Adler, *Guidance and Counselling: Principles and Techniques* (MEd Notes, Madurai Kamaraj University Package 12, 1982) 35.
4. *Ibid*, 35.
5. Paulose Mar Gregorious, *The Human Presence*: (Madras: The Christian Literature Society, 1980, 75-76.
6. *Paulose Mar Gregorious*, 76.
7. John Wilson Foster, *Criss and Ritual in Brian Moore's Belfast Novels Eire-Ireland*, (Autmn 1968) 67.
8. Paulose Mar Gregorious, *op.cit.*, 92.

BIBLIOGRAPHY

A. PRIMARY SOURCES

a) Graham Greene

Greene, Graham. *The Man Within*. 1929, Harmondsworth: Penguin, 1977.

Greene, Graham. *It's a Battlefield*. 1934, Harmondsworth: Penguin, 1977.

Greene, Graham. *England Made Me*. 1935, Harmondsworth: Penguin, 1977.

Greene, Graham. *A Gun for Sale*. 1936, Harmondsworth: Penguin, 1975.

Greene, Graham. *Journey Without Maps*. 1936, Harmondsworth: Penguin, 1978.

Greene, Graham. *Brighton Rock*. 1938, Harmondsworth: Penguin, 1977.

Greene, Graham. *The Lawless Roads*. 1939, Harmondsworth: Penguin, 1976.

Greene, Graham. *The Power and the Glory*. 1943, Harmondsworth: Penguin, 1967.

Greene, Graham. *The Ministry of Fear*. 1943. Harmondsworth: Penguin, 1976.

Greene, Graham. *The Heart of the Matter*. 1948, Harmondsworth: Penguin, 1977.

Greene, Graham. *The Quiet American* 1955, Harmondsworth: Penguin, 1977.

Greene, Graham. *Our Man in Havana* 1958, Harmondsworth: Penguin, 1978.

Greene, Graham. *A Burnt-out Case* 1961, Harmondsworth: Penguin, 1977.

Greene, Graham. *The Potting Shed*. 1958, Harmondsworth: Penguin, 1977.

Greene, Graham. *Travels with My Aunt*. 1969, Harmondsworth: Penguin, 1977.

Greene, Graham. *A Sort of Life*. 1970, Harmondsworth: Penguin, 1977.

Greene, Graham. *The Honorary Consul*. 1973, Harmondsworth: Penguin, 1975.

Greene, Graham. *The Human Factor*. 1978, New York: Avon Books, 1978.

Greene, Graham. *Ways of Escape*. London: The Bodley Head, 1989.

Greene, Graham. *Monsignor Quixote*. 1982, Harmondsworth: Penguin, 1983.

b) Brian Moore

Moore, Brian. *Judith Hearne*. 1955, Boston: Little Brown 1956.

Moore, Brian. *The Feast of Lupercal*. 1957, London: Andre Deutsch, 1960.

Moore, Brian. *An Answer from Limbo*. 1962: London: Andre Deutsch, 1963.

Moore, Brian. *The Emperor of Ice-Cream*. London: Andre Deutsch, 1963.

Moore, Brian. *I am Mary Dunne*. London: Jonathan Cape. 1968.

Moore, Brian. *Fergus*. 1970, London: Jonathan Cape, 1971.

Moore, Brian. *The Revolution Script*. 1971, London: Jonathan Cape, 1972.

Moore, Brian. *Catholics*. London: Jonathan Cape, 1972.

Moore, Brian. *The Great Victorian Collection*: London: Jonathan Cape, 1975.

Moore, Brian. The Doctor's Wife. London: Jonathan Cape, 1976.

Moore, Brian. The Mangan Inheritance. London: Jonathan Cape, 1979.

Moore, Brian. The Temptation of Eileen Hughes. London: Jonathan Cape, 1981.

Moore, Brian. Cold Heaven, London: Jonathan Cape, 1983.

Moore, Brian. The Colour of Blood. London: Jonathan Cape, 1987.

Moore, Brian. List of Silence. London: Bloomsburg, 1990.

3. SECONDARY SOURCES

Abbot, Walter M. ed. *The Documents of Vatican II*. New York: The American Press, 1966.

Abrams, M.H. *Literature and Belief*, New York: New York, 1958.

Alice, Rev. Sr. *Mary Newman and the Oxford Movement*. Trivandrum: Printers Combines, 1983.

Allport, G.W. *The Individual and His Religion*, New York: Macmillan, 1960.

Allott, Kenneth and Miriam Farris. *The Art of Graham Greene*, New York: Russel and Russel, 1963.

Atkins, John. *Graham Greene*, London: John Calder, 1957.

Bown, Elizabeth et al. *Why do I Write: An exchange of Views between Elizabeth Bowen*, Graham Greene and V.S. Pritchet. USA: Cloth Haskel P, 1982.

Bradburg, Malcoem, ed. *The Novel Today*. Fontana: Collins, 1978.

Burges, Anthony, *The New Novel*. London: Faber, 1967.

Coomaraswamy, *Ananda K. What is Civilisation*. New Delhi: Oxford, 1989.

Coomaraswamy, *The Christian and Oriental Philosophy of Art*. New Delhi: Munshiram Manoharlal, 1974.

Clark, W.H. *The Psychology of Religion*. New York: Macmillan, 1959.

Clarke, Waldo. *A Short History of English Literature*, London: Nigeria Pub, 1979.

Dalhie, Hallvard. *Brian Moore*. Toronto: Copp Clark, 1969.

Durant, Will. *The Story of Philosophy*. New York: Washington Square. 1961.

Evely, Louis. *Suffering*. London: Burns of Oates, 1968.

Flood, Jeanne M. *Brian Moore*. Pennsylvania: Bucknell UP, 1974.

Ford, Boris, ed. *The New Pelican Guide to English Literature* (Vol. 7), Harmondsworth: Penguin, 1985.

Gregorious Mar Paulose. *Swathanthriya Deepthi*. Madras: The Christian Literature Society, 1971.

Ghosh Aurobindo. *The Future Poetry*. Pondicherry: Sri Aurobindo Ashram, 1991.

Hynes, Samuel, ed. *Graham Greene. A Collection of Critical Essays*. New Jersey: Prentice Hall, 1993.

Ivasheva, *V. Twentieth Century English Literature: A Soviet View*. Moscow: Progress Publishers, 1982.

Iyengar, Sreenivas. *Adventure of Literary Criticism*, New Delhi: Sterling, 1985.

James, William. *The Varieties of Religious Experience*, London: Longman's 1952.

Jeremy, Hawthorn. *Studying the Novel: an Introduction*. New Delhi: Ansari, 1991.

Joseph, Jastrow. *Freud His Dream and Sex Theories*, New York: Perma, 1959.

Kettle, Arnold. *An Introduction to the English Novel*. London: Hutchinson, 1967.

Kermode, Frank. *Literary Fiction and Reality*. Harmondsworth: Penguin, 1973

Kulshrestha, J.P. *Graham Greene: His Mind and Art*. Delhi: Sterling, 1987.

Lewis, R.W.B. *The Picaresque Saint*. London: Victor Gollancz, 1960.

Lioddell, Robert. *A Treatise on the Novel*. London: Cape, 1965.

Lodge, David. *The Novelist at the Crossroads*, London: Routledge 1971.

Mesnet, Marie Beatrice. *Graham Greene and The Heart of the Matter*. London: The Cresset, 1954.

Nithya Chaithanya Yatni. *Kala Sahithya Saparya*. Konni: Venus 1988.

Nithya Chaithanya Yathi. *Psychology in Life*. *Kottayam*. D.C. 1992.

O' Donoghue, Jo. *Brian Moore: A Critical Study*, Montreal: McGill UP, 1991.

Paul, Edwards (ed). *The Encyclopedia of Philosophy*, New York: Collier-Macmillan, 1972.

Pryce-Jones, David. *Graham Greene*. London: Oliver and Boyd, 1966.

Rai, Gangeshwar. *Graham Greene. An Existential Approach*, New Delhi: Associated Publishing House, 1985.

Raven, Charles. *Theilhard de Chardin*. New York: Harper and Row, 1962.

Russel, Bernard. *Mysticism and Logic*. London: Allen and Unwin, 1963.

Sartre, Jean-Paul. *Being and Nothingness*. New York: Washington Square P, 1966.

Schwartz, Herman S. *The Art of Relaxation*. Bombay: Jaico, 1991.

Seturaman, V.S., ed *Contemporary Criticism: An Anthology*, New Delhi: Macmillan, 1989.

Sherry, Nornam. *Life of Graham Greene*. Harmondsworth: Penguin, 1990.

Smith, Grahame. *The Achievement of Graham Greene*. Susex: The Harvester, 1986.

Spurling, John. *Graham Greene. London: Methuen*, 1983.

Stratford, Philip, ed. *The Portable Graham Greene*. Harmondsworth: Penguin, 1977.

Subramanyam, K.S. *Graham Greene: A Study*. Bareilly: Prakash, 1978.

Tagore, Rabindranath. *The Creative Unity*. Madras: Macmillan, 1971.

Tharakan, K.M. *The Poetic Act*. New Delhi: Macmillan, 1978.

West, Paul. *The Modern Novel*. London: Hutchinson, 1963.

Wilf, Wilkinson. *To me Personally*. London: Collins, 1972.

Wyndam, Francis. *Graham Greene*. Essex: Longman, 1977.

ARTICLES

Braybrooke, Neville. "Graham Greene – The Double Man. An Approach to his Novel, The End of the Affair, *Queens Quarterly*, 77. Spring (1920): 29-39.

Foster, John Wilson. "Crisis and Ritual in Brian Moore's Belfast Novels", *Eire-Ireland*, Autumn, (1968) 56-74.

French, Philip. "The Novels of Brian Moore". *London Magazine* Feb. (1960): 85-91.

Gallagher, Michael Paul. 'Brian Moore's Fiction of Faith," *Gaeliana* 5, (1985) 94.

Harley, Michael. "The Problem of Original Sin" *The Clergy Review* 52. No 10 (October 1967), 770-85.

Henry, Dewitt, "The Novels of Brian Moore a Retrospective", *Ploughshares* 2 (1974) 7-26.

Huxley, Sir Julian. "The New Divinity", *The Twentieth Century*, 170. Autumn (1961): 9-18.

Less, F.N. "Graham Greene: A Comment" *Scrutiny*, 19, October (1952): 31-42.

Hortmann, Wilhelm. "Graham Greene: The Burnt-out Catholic". *Twentieth Century Literature*. 10 July (1964): 64-76.

Lewis, R.W.B. "The Trilogy of Graham Greene." *Modern Fiction Studies*, 3, Autumn (1957): 3.

Lewis, R.W.B. "The Fiction of Graham Greene: Between the Horror and the Glory." *The Kenyon Review*, 19, N Winter (1957): 56-75.

Martin, Guy. "Interview with Graham Greene", *Realities Christmas Issue*, (1962): 60-63.

McSweeney, Kerry. *Brian Moore: Past and Present, Critical Quarterly*, 18, Summer, (1976): 53-66.

McDonald, James L. "Graham Greene: A Reconsideration." Arizona Quarterly, Autumn (1971): 27.

Noxon, James. Kierkegaards Stages and A Burnt-out Case A Rev. of English Literature, 3, January, (1962): 90-101.

Pattern, Karl. "The Structure of the Power and the Glory." *Modern Fiction Studies*, 3, Autumn (1957): 225-34.

Ricks, Christopher. The Simple Excellence of Brian Moore, *The New Statesman* 71 Feb, (1966): 227-8.

Rolo, Charles. "Graham Greene: The Man and the Message." *Atlantic Monthly*, May (1961): 60-65.

Smith, A.J.M. "Graham Greene's Theological Thrillers." *Queen's Quarterly*, 68 Spring (1961): 15-33.

Stratford, Philip. "Unlocking the Potting Shed." *The Kenyon Review*, 24, Winter (1962): 129-43.

Weatherby, W.J. "Voyage to Greeneland". *The Guardian*, 14 October (1979): 4.

Wichert, Robert A. "The Quality of Graham Greene's Mercy, *College English*, 25, November (1963): 99-103.

Woodcock, George. *Away from Lost Worlds: Notes on the Development of Canadian Literature*, Commonwealth Literature 209-20, Oxford: Clarendon, (1973): 209-20.

INDEX